THE CONQUEROR'S CITY

Although modern Alexandria stands right on the site of ancient Alexandria hardly any of the Alexandria known to the ancients remains. But a great deal is known of this old city and nearby Pharos island which was the site of one of the Seven Wonders of the ancient world—the Pharos lighthouse.

Ancient Alexandria was founded and received its name from Alexander the Great in 332 B.C. and, although Alexander did not see its completion, he was buried there. Many other famous people were also connected with it.

Among these was Cleopatra, who built the magnificent temple of Caesareum in honour of Mark Anthony and adorned it with two obelisks, one of which now stands on the Embankment, London, and the other in Central Park, New York. The Caesareum and the obelisks are shown in the picture, which is an artist's impression of what Alexandria may have looked like in ancient Roman times.

Famous Alexandrian scholars, known today throughout the world, are Euclid, the geometrician, Eratosthenes, the geographer and Hipparchus, the astronomer.

Mark Anthony, the Emperor Caracalla and Hadrian studied at the old library at Alexandria, although the library was burned down during the time of Julius Caesar and around 750,000 manuscripts were destroyed. Another library was founded shortly afterwards, however, with 200,000 works given to Cleopatra by Mark Anthony.

Present-day Alexandria is a modern and carefully planned city but it is probably nowhere near as wonderful to modern eyes as old Alexandria must have been to the ancients.

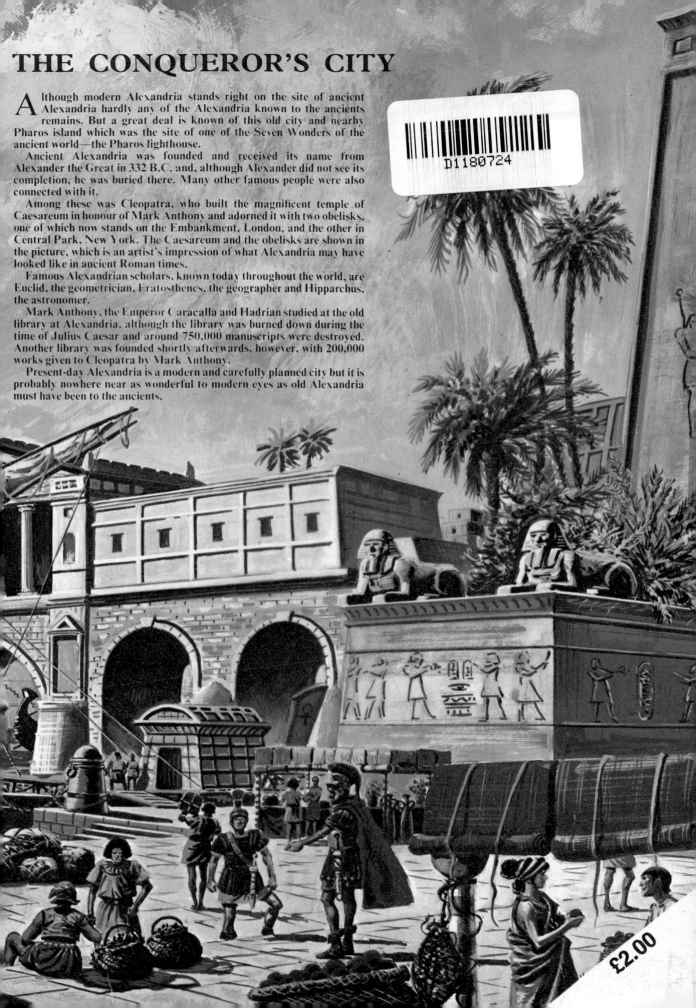

£2.00

FROM THE SOURCE TO THE SEA

...The Story Of A River

Millions of years ago, most of the hills and mountains in the British Isles were forced upwards from under the sea by enormous earth movements. The geological strata is formed from materials such as chalk, clay, limestone and sand. Rain water soaks through the permeable layers, but on reaching impervious clay or sandstone the water travels along until it emerges as a spring.

Molten igneous rock forced its way into the great folds which formed in the early crust of the Earth. This molten rock burst through fissures, leaving cracks in the surface. Millions of years later, rain soaked through the chalk and sand layers on the sides of the hill and was stopped by the sandstone. The water seeped through the sides and flowed over the fissure as a waterfall.

Where a spring emerges near a road or village, it may be utilised to fill a horse trough or to serve as a village pump.

Rock-strewn rapids are formed when a river erodes its way through soft strata. When rushing water wears down rock to form a ravine, different strata in the rock faces are exposed. Geologists in search of fossils, such as ammonites (right), find such places ideal hunting grounds.

HYDRAULIC RAM

UNDERGROUND PIPE SUPPLYING FARM

WASTE OUTLET

STICKLEBACK

GREY WAGTAIL

GOLDEN PLOVER

Few rivers have a recognisable source because usually several small rivulets join together at the start and these are often quite dry until rain falls. When a large spring does burst forth to create the single source of a river, this may continue flowing at an almost constant rate throughout the year.

As the water forms a stream, it may soon encounter a cliff and pour over as a waterfall. Such cliffs were created either as "faults" when large sections of rock cracked away and sank, or by the action of the water eroding away some softer material adjacent to the rock. Over thousands of years, the rushing water may have worn down the rock to form a ravine, making rapids instead of a waterfall. One can then see the different strata exposed in the rock faces; such a spot is an ideal one to hunt for fossils.

Man found the upland hills suitable for sheep farming. When walking along a stream in such country, you may come across old stone or brick walls lining the banks. This may be a sheepwash. By penning water in the trough and driving the

The hydraulic ram system of pumping water to high ground is both cheap and effective, as it uses the movement of the water as fuel. Above right can be seen some of the creatures to be found in the upland river country.

sheep through, the fleeces were washed just prior to shearing. Similar structures were also used to dip the sheep to keep insects off their wool. Modern detergents and chemicals have largely ousted these methods.

As the farmyard was often sited on high ground away from the river, man had to devise a simple way to get water for drinking and washing to the house. Deep wells sunk into the "aquifer" (water-bearing stratum) were used in early times. Later on, windmill pumps were used, and from the middle of the 19th century the hydraulic ram became popular, running indefinitely and at no cost as the movement of the water was used as fuel. These automatic pumps are still in use, and you will know when

NATURAL VALLEY

STRATA

EROSION

RIVER

CLIFF

RIFT VALLEY   FAULT

RIVER

The diagrams on the left represent two types of river valley. The natural valley was formed by the river cutting its own bed. In ancient times it was much wider. The lower diagram illustrates a dramatic subsidence in the earth in prehistoric times. Rift valleys have distinctive cliffs and flat floors.

WATER-MILL

MILL RACE

LEVEL ARTIFICIAL MILLSTREAM

CATTLE BRIDGE

NATURAL RIVER COURSE

A typical site for a water-mill.

The kingfisher and the rainbow trout are just two of the creatures that can be seen along the upper reaches of a river.

Timber-felling was an important industry in the days when oak was needed for shipbuilding and the wood was transported down river. The top branches of the trees were converted into charcoal.

GRAYLING

DACE

Right, a typical reservoir constructed of concrete on a rock base. Reservoirs are used for the generation of electric power and for irrigation as well as for general water supply. Above are two fish which can be found in the fast-flowing middle reaches of the river.

you have found one because you will see a small brickwork chamber with a trap door on top, and you will hear a loud click from inside every second or two.

Near the source, there will be few fish of any size, but sticklebacks and similar minnows may succumb to the enthusiast's net. Many interesting species of birds should be seen by the patient observer, including the golden plover and the grey wagtail. Types of trees depend greatly upon the nature of the soil, but conifers such as larch, spruce and scots fir are likely.

We now follow the flow of water as it collects various small tributaries and traces the lowest levels through a valley.

A ravine of narrow width has probably been cut by the river during recent times, though "recent" in geological language

This illustration shows a fish ladder which enables fish to jump in easy stages to the top of a dam.

FISH LADDER

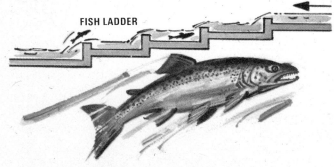

may mean more than a thousand years!

If you examine a small river which runs through a valley over half a kilometre wide, you may depend on it that this was formed by glaciers in the Ice Age, or at an even earlier time when land masses were quite different from now and when this river was perhaps one hundred times its present size. If there are vertical cliffs (or "bluffs") at the sides, you may have found a rift valley, created by a colossal subsidence in the earth.

Man has made full use of the way in which a river flows through a valley. An ideal site for a water-mill occurred where the river flowed close to a hillside, then meandered away down the valley and once again looped close to the same hillside. By cutting a level millstream along the hill contour and diverting water into it, a "head" of 3 to 6 metres was formed, possessing great power to turn a big paddle wheel. The spent water then flowed back into the original course at the lower loop.

Where mills were sited, a village often grew up, and other industries collected. Nowadays, you may find a sizable town there.

Walking along the banks of a river set in a wide valley with pasture land each side, you may come across a weir, or a penstock. Both serve the same purpose: to raise the level of the water in order to provide safe drinking places for cattle, to form a deep water "fence" which prevents cattle from straying or to enable pumps to withdraw water for irrigation or drinking.

Weirs are fixed barriers forming artificial waterfalls. Penstocks have fixed side walls with, in early instances, removable boards between them working in slots and enabling the water to be released in flood time. Modern penstocks have metal gates with winding mechanisms, some operating automatically according to the height of the water.

Trout fishing may be possible on this reach of the river.

Trout like fast flowing streams with occasional pools, but where the bed is muddy, there may be eels. Long ago, men built

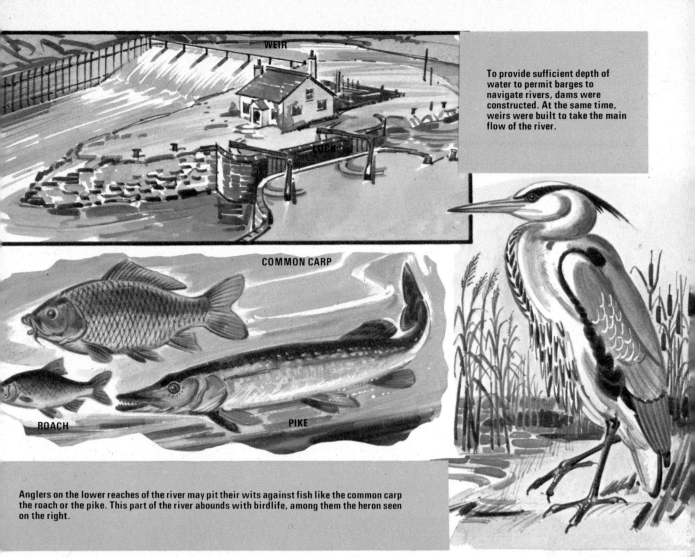

WEIR

LOCK

COMMON CARP

ROACH

PIKE

Anglers on the lower reaches of the river may pit their wits against fish like the common carp the roach or the pike. This part of the river abounds with birdlife, among them the heron seen on the right.

eel traps into the sides of weirs and at water-mills, and one can still find these intact. Water was allowed to flow from the higher level into a large chamber discharging through an orifice at the bottom. A wicker cage was left at the bottom and when this was pulled up on a rope, there was a good chance of finding many fine eels trapped inside.

The bed-gradient of most rivers alters throughout their length so that the water runs more and more slowly as it approaches the sea. Fast-flowing water picks up mud and sand, but these materials settle where the flow is slower, only to be moved again in flood time.

Along the middle reaches, there is often silt and sand to considerable depths on the bed. Sand has evolved from the slow erosion of sandstone rocks, and from Roman times men have dredged sand from rivers to use for making plaster and mortar.

Today, sand is in great demand for use in concrete-mixing and in making sand-faced bricks.

Timber brought prosperity to many a river hundreds of years ago, because floating logs down the river was much simpler than haulage over land, even if this meant waiting for a flush of rain-water. Before steam sawmills became common early in the 19th century, all logs had to be cut into planks by hand-operated pit saws. Charcoal-burning was often carried out near rivers by itinerant workers. Alder trees are frequently found along river banks, and this kind of wood was considered the best for making charcoal for use in gunpowder.

The most common riverside trees in England are alder and willow but oak, ash, poplar and hornbeam like this location too.

With the growing demand for water in the towns, more dams are being built across river valleys to create reservoirs. Sometimes buildings and trees are submerged in the process. Suitable sites are difficult to find, since the valley must be narrow where the dam is built, while the geological strata must be suitable both for taking the weight of the dam and for preventing loss of water by seepage. Big reservoirs may affect the livelihoods of many people, but there are advantages as far

as recreation is concerned if the expanses of water can be made available for dinghy-racing and fishing.

Nature-lovers will find much of interest along the middle reaches. They will almost certainly see moorhens and coot, and perhaps swans, voles, otters and even wild mink. Botanists can collect varieties of water weeds, kingcups, rushes, water lilies and flags.

The lower reaches can be said to be the start of stretches which can readily be used for navigation. High land is normally some distance from the river, and the adjacent plains are composed of alluvium, sand, or clay which was laid down by water-action millions of years ago.

Peat is also most likely to occur in these areas. Nowadays it is used only in a small way as fuel, but peat digging is still an industry because peat is used in horticultural work.

Peat is composed of layer upon layer of rotting vegetation but, being normally near the surface, it has not become compressed into a hard material like coal.

Where the lower reaches flow through these alluvial plains, they tend to meander in curves. Erosion makes these meanders more pronounced over the years, and a really large loop may become bypassed, eventually forming an "ox-bow" lake. Reeds and rushes proliferate in these lakes and become nesting grounds for mallard, teal, and other species of wild duck.

During the 18th and 19th centuries, water-transport became the main method of moving heavy loads such as timber, coal, chalk, stone, wheat, flour, hay, straw and iron. Locks were constructed to provide sufficient depths of water for loaded barges. Each lock required a weir to take the flow of the river, and oxbow lakes were often utilised when constructing these.

Only a few of our larger rivers are used now for commercial navigation, but you may find when walking along the banks of many rivers the remains of old timber wharfs in some quite isolated areas.

The loss of land eroded by rivers has always been a problem, and along the middle reaches you may find certain places where old barges have been sunk along the edge of the river to prevent the banks slipping away.

The river authorities carry out revetment works with stone, chalk, timber, steel piling and concrete. The old methods in which hazel faggots or fascine (long faggot) mattresses were staked and wired to the foreshore are still used in some districts.

Trees may not be numerous along the lower reaches, but there may be a variety of flora and fauna in and close to the river. The variety of fishes depends very largely upon the velocity of the water, but there could well be carp, roach, sea trout, pike as well as other species.

Approaching The Sea

When the river leaves the lower reaches, it rapidly approaches the sea.

This stretch is the estuary, which can be defined roughly as that length of the river which is influenced by the tides.

Tidal embankments are usually constructed along the sides of the estuary to prevent high tides overflowing on to adjacent farmland. Until comparatively recent years, this land was marshland, and high tides usually overflowed it. This is why this soil is usually composed of silt on top of alluvium or clay.

Man started to reclaim these marshlands in the Middle Ages, and near some estuaries can be seen the remains of ancient earthen embankments which were originally used to surround somebody's land.

As time passed, these embankments were moved to the edge of the main river course. In them you will find sluices through which ditches can flow. On the river side, these sluices have tidal flap valves to prevent the tidal water flowing through on to the land.

The early sluices were made of brick and timber, but today they are made of concrete, with metal valves. Some of them have penstocks which allow the farmers to hold water in the ditches during dry weather.

Rarely is there a shortage of fish in an estuary. Flat fish like flounders are usually present in the mud or sand; and many sea fish like grey mullet and bass travel up wtih the tide at certain times of the year. Eels are usually numerous, and are easy to catch.

Bird life in these areas is interesting and varied. Lapwings, redshanks, curlews and other waders, and the black-headed gull can all be seen.

A wind-powered land drainage pump. At one time these were used frequently in Holland and in East Anglia.

One method used for raising land drainage water is the ancient Archimedes screw principle. In olden days, oxen were used to rotate the screw, but nowadays electric motors are used. Much marshland has been reclaimed in the river estuary areas by this and other means of drainage.

BLACK-HEADED GULL

SANDPIPER CURLEW

LAPWING

Right, some of the birds which may be found in the locality of the estuary.

8

Because they offer a limitless supply of cooling water, estuaries are ideal sites for power stations. Conservationists are always concerned to see that these and other large industries do not spoil peoples' enjoyment of the river by polution.

When the estuary of a big river merges with the sea, it may be over 1.5 kilometres wide, so the actual mouth of the river can be difficult to define.

However, many smaller rivers join the sea quite abruptly and more often than not there will be a small port, perhaps more than one, at the mouth. Such ports started centuries ago as no more than groups of fishermen's cottages, but as populations increased, wharves were constructed to facilitate the loading and unloading of goods from cargo ships. Later on, shipbuilding and other industries sprang up in some of these places.

Where a river meets the sea, the speed of its flow is rapidly decreased and this allows sand and silt to sink to the sea bed. An accumulation of this can form an obstacle to deep-draught ships, and to eliminate these shoals most ports have harbour walls or moles running out to sea. They create a length of channel which can be dredged when required.

To prevent the sea breaking through these harbour works, groynes or dunes have to be maintained along the beaches. In earlier days, groynes were often built of bundles of brushwood called "faggots". Nowadays, timber piles supporting planking are favoured.

Marram grass is planted in the sand dunes to increase their size. These dunes form a fine natural barrier against the sea.

Upstream from the river mouth, saltings can frequently be found. These are mud flats submerged by high tides, and are usually covered with grass and other herbage. In them there will often be small creeks which are sometimes used by yachtsmen, to lay up their boats in the winter.

Moorings for yachts will be found near the mouths of most rivers. Sailing is now so popular that in many places there is insufficient space for future moorings, and schemes are afoot to build marinas or yacht harbours which can accommodate hundreds of small craft in a minimum of space. By excavating saltings, marinas can sometimes be constructed without the loss of valuable land.

Since rivers are so important for future recreation, great efforts are being made to prevent these areas from becoming spoilt. Unfortunately, such areas make good sites for nuclear and coal-fired electricity generating stations because the supplies of cooling water are limitless. Other industries such as oil refineries also prefer seaside locations.

The Royal Yachting Association fights constantly to preserve sailing amenities for the future, and they have successfully prevented the closure of many rivers by overhead cables, fixed road bridges and other obstacles.

Close to the river mouth, there may be a wide variety of fish such as bass, herring, skate and mackerel. Offshore fishermen with deep-sea motor-cruisers may find cod, tope, conger, small sharks and other line-breaking specimens!

Throughout the year many birds can be seen, including shoreline waders such as dunlins, oyster catchers, sanderlings, and knots. Cormorants, puffins and herring gulls may be found farther out to sea, or near a rocky shore.

Intriguing types of jelly fish can also be seen floating near the surface. A word of warning, though! It is wise not to touch these, since some of them can sting quite badly, particularly the Portuguese man-o'-war, which carries its own sail above water.

Right, a typical small yacht repair yard, an industry which flourishes at the mouth of most rivers. The skate and the conger eel are among the wide variety of fish to be found at the mouth of the river. The cormorant is just one of the many birds that makes its home in the area.

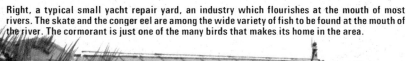

Where sea and river meet, sand and silt inevitably form bars which obstruct large ships. To prevent this, most ports have harbour walls running out to create an extended channel which can easily be dredged. But even these harbour works have to be protected, and one of the best ways of doing this is by maintaining groynes (wooden fences) along the beach.

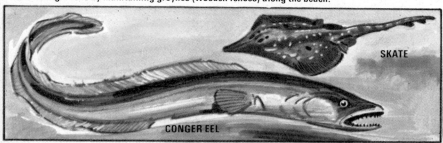

SKATE

CONGER EEL

CHEATS HAD A HARD TIME IN OLYMPIA

IT was always crowded in the city of Olympia at the time of the Olympic Games. Plato, the Greek philosopher, complained bitterly that he had to share a tent with another visitor who reeked of garlic.

The games, held every four years, just as they are now, were a summertime event. That was because in summer there was always less work for the Greeks to do in the fields and also because it was the best season of the year to travel.

The athletes had to assemble in Olympia at least a month before the games. There was a gymnasium in which they could practise, a couple of hundred metres from the stadium.

The call summoning them to the games went out several months before the events. It was a call for a truce, for all wars were suspended during the games' period. The Greeks hung up their spears and shields with weary relief and converged excitedly upon the city-state of Olympia.

For a Greek in ancient times there was no greater honour than to win an event at the Olympiad. It was a prize far more greatly cherished than any commendation for bravery in battle. Because of this, some athletes cheated. The commonest form of cheating was giving – or accepting – bribe money.

There was a terrible penalty paid by those found out. They were first heavily fined and if they couldn't pay their city-state – Sparta, Corinth, Athens, for example – had to pay for them. Then a statue was made of the cheat and his name fixed to it. The statue was placed just outside the Olympic stadium, where all who went to the games could see it, to the criminal's everlasting shame.

When in the last century archaeologists excavated Olympia, they found the bases of sixteen cheats' statues. As the Greeks will tell you today, that didn't mean that there were only sixteen cheats, but rather that only sixteen of them were caught.

The stadium itself was 198 metres long. All Greek stadia were supposed to be 600 feet long, but since the people who paced them out all had different size feet, the stadia all varied in size. That at Delphi, for instance, came out at only 178 metres.

Women didn't participate in the games and women – with one exception – were not even allowed to watch. The

Above: Entrance to the world's oldest Olympic Stadium. Below: Ruins of the gymnasium, where competitors trained before the Olympics.

All that is left of the Temple of Hera, built about 650 B.C.

A temple terrace where once athletes made offerings to the gods.

exception was the high priestess of the goddess Demeter, mother of the earth, for whom a special seat was kept opposite the judges.

The games, which were first held 776 years before the birth of Christ, were considered so sacred and so important that even the spectators had to be free men – no slaves were allowed in – and those who had been convicted of any crime were forbidden to watch.

There were 40,000 spectators, and they reclined on the grassy banks overlooking the track. There were no seats or grandstands at the Olympic stadium.

The events were remarkably varied. One race was 24 times the length of the stadium (long-distance competitors ran back and forth, not round the stadium as they do today). There was a pentathlon (jumping, discus-throwing, javelin, foot-racing and wrestling); boxing contests and boys' events.

The games lasted five days and on the sixth day a young boy was deputed to cut a branch from an olive tree. The leaves were fashioned into wreaths and placed on the heads of the victors in a moving ceremony.

The Olympic Stadium. Competitors ran up and down, and spectators sat on the grass banks.

12

Steps and fallen slabs: the ruins of the Temple of Zeus, one of the seven Wonders of the World.

Left: Foot of a column from the great Temple of Zeus. Below: Pillars of the gymnasium.

It was their deep sense of honour through physical strength and the nobility of athletic competition that inspired the Greeks to strive and win, and caused their enemies to envy them. A Greek writer tells us of a group of Greek soldiers who deserted after a battle and joined the Persians.

One of the Greeks explained to the Persians that in Olympia athletic contests were held every four years.

Xerses, the Persian king who was listening, asked: "What reward is given to the winners?"

"A wreath made from a wild olive branch," replied one of the Greeks.

At this a Persian officer said to his King: "Alas, sir, that we should have to make war on such people as the Greeks. For these are men who fight not for wealth, but for virtue."

The city-state of Olympia was twice blessed, for besides the Olympic stadium it was also the home of one of the seven wonders of the ancient world. This was the great statue of Zeus, the supreme Greek god, who sat on a golden throne inside a huge Temple of Zeus.

The statue – seven times larger than life size – was fashioned in gold and ivory by Pheidias, the Michelangelo of the ancient Greek world. It was he who designed the great Parthenon on the Acropolis of Athens.

Pheidias set up a workshop across the road from the Temple. Centuries later, when Olympia was a ruin, the Byzantine Greeks turned that workshop into a Christian church. That, too, is now one of the ruins of Olympia.

The great statue was crowned with a silver olive wreath. In its right hand it held a gold and ivory figure of Victory; in its left a sceptre supporting an eagle.

It sat on a gold, jewel-encrusted throne and must have been in total a glittering sight. But we are told that more marvellous than all the precious gems that adorned the statue was its expression of calm kindliness – an expression that apparently inspired the faithful pilgrims to greater devotion. An ancient Greek poet was so moved by the statue that he told Pheidias: "You must have gone to heaven to see Zeus."

A few metres outside the main doorway to the great Temple of Zeus was a huge pile of ashes 22 metres high. These were the ashes of animals sacrificed by visitors to the Temple. The outside of the lower layers was built up in such a way that worshippers could ascend steps to reach the top of the pile and continue to make sacrificed. Where the pile of ashes once stood there is today a hollow depression in the ground.

Olympia, like much of mainland Greece, was plagued by earthquakes and it was an earthquake, we are told, that finally destroyed the city. But in fact there may not have been much of the city left to destroy when that calamity befell it in the sixth century A.D.

For in the year 394 A.D. Theodocius the First, Emperor of the Eastern Roman Empire and a Christian, abolished the Olympic games because, he said, they were a pagan festival. In that same year the great statue of Zeus, that wonder of the world, was taken off to Theodocius capital at Constantinople.

Twenty-six years later Theodocius the Second ordered that the deserted Temple should be burned. "It's a pagan place, and it's quite wrong that we Christians should allow it to stand," he told his subjects.

So the Temple was burned and in the next century two earthquakes threw the remaining bits about. It was a sad end for the masterpiece that people had once travelled from all over the Mediterranean world to see.

For 1500 years Olympia's ruins lay buried under the earth. When they were excavated, the finds included 1,300 objects made of gold and 130 statues.

The re-discovery of Olympia fired the imagination of a French baron, Pierre de Coubertin, whose suggestion it was that the Olympic Games should be revived.

THE ROAMING ROMANIES

THE Gypsy way of life is very different from that of most people. Instead of living in permanent homes, Gypsies travel about the country, belong to clans, and have their own secret language and laws. Many people are biased against them. If any trouble has occurred in their area, these people are always ready to believe that it is the Gypsies who are at fault. Sometimes, of course, they are; they would be less than human if they were not.

Other people, more tolerant of the Gypsies, are very friendly towards them. For the old, romantic ideas of Gypsy life still linger on.

We think of gaily painted caravans, the scent of wood smoke from a camp fire, old Gypsy women with clay pipes between their lips, and handsome men playing thrilling melodies on the violin, while gaily dressed Gypsy girls dance to the light of the fires and the moon.

There are fragments of truth in this picture also, though such sights are much less common, at least in Britain, than they were at the beginning of this century, when the motor car was a novelty, and the fastest traffic on most roads was the vehicle drawn by a horse.

The selling, handling, and care of horses was still the Gypsy's main occupation, and the great reduction in the number of horses used in transport and for farming during the past fifty years has made it much harder for a Gypsy to make a living in the way he used to.

Where do the Gypsies come from? Nobody knows for certain. They do not readily talk about themselves to strangers, and have their own secret signs, customs, and language. In the last few years there have been many books about them, but in spite of what we can learn from these, the Gypsies still guard many of their secrets.

The true Gypsy rarely calls himself by that name. To his own people he is a "Rom", which in Gypsy language means just "Man". That is why Gypsies are often called "Romanies". All other people they call "Gadjes" or "Gorgios". But not everyone who leads a wandering life is a true Gypsy and in some countries – especially in southern Spain – even the genuine Rom no longer travels around, but lives in a house, or perhaps a comfortably furnished cave!

Gypsy men gained a reputation as clever horse dealers and even horse doctors and many of the women claimed to have powers of fortune-telling. This picture shows a typical market place during the middle of the 18th century in Britain where gypsies displayed their talents at horse-dealing, music-making and fortune-telling.

This picture shows a gypsy family in the middle of the 19th century with their beautifully decorated home on wheels.

In Britain there are about fifty thousand people who are described as Gypsies, but of these, only about one in every five is a true Rom, and it is about this mysterious people that we are now concerned. The names given to them by others show how little is known of their true history. For "Gypsy" is a short form of "Egyptian" and for a long time it was believed that it was from Egypt that they came to Europe. In Turkey they are known as 'Fawrani' (Pharaoh's people) – another way of saying that they came from Egypt! The Dutch call them "Heiden" (Heathen), the Spanish, "Gitanos" suggesting Egypt again as their first homeland.

It is almost certain that they came in the first place from much farther East. Their language closely resembles the language of ancient India called Sanskrit, and many people say that it was in some part of North India that they first began their wanderings, many centuries ago, and that they have been roving the world ever since. Some scholars fix their first homeland more exactly, in the Hindu Kush, a

wild, inhospitable region of what today we call Afghanistan.

It is thought that they fled westward to escape the terrible invasion of the Mongols, led by the tyrant Tamerlane in the fourteenth century. There are records of Gypsies camping on Luneberg Heath in central Germany, as early as 1417.

But there is always the possibility that they came even earlier, as a tribe of musicians who were brought from India to the Royal Court of Persia in 420 A.D., and from Persia slowly moved by way of Turkey, Greece, and the Balkan States, into Western Europe. This could well account for the well-known skill as dancers and musicians which many of them still display.

By the year 1500 they were coming to England in ever-growing numbers, and soon began to use other skills for which they are still renowned. The Gypsy men knew far more about horses than did the average English countryman, and soon gained a name as clever horse dealers, and even as horse doctors. The Gypsies were also

skilled workers in metal, and although not all tinkers are Gypsies, many Gypsies made a living by repairing damaged pans and kettles.

We tend to think of Gypsies as lonely travellers, just a man, his family, a dog, a horse and a caravan. But every Gypsy is in fact very much aware of belonging to a "Clan" or "Tribe", and if travelling alone will most probalby be on his way to meet other members of his tribe. Within each tribe there is a very strong feeling of loyalty between members, who will travel many miles to visit even a distant cousin if he or she is ill, and to attend the funeral if one has died. A Gypsy's wife will almost certainly be of the same tribe as her husband, for there are many differences of custom and behaviour between the different tribes, and marriage between members of different tribes is frowned upon.

The very worse thing that can happen to a Gypsy is to be expelled from his own tribe. Such a fate may be rare, and only enforced in the case of some serious wrong or injury done to an innocent member of the tribe. Such cases never come before our ordinary Courts of Law. They are decided entirely by the "Elders" of the tribe concerned.

The Elders are a small group of older men who have been appointed by the tribe to act as judges in matters of Gypsy Law. They hold their own courts, often in the open air, always in secret, and their decision is accepted as final by the whole tribe after they have heard what all the people involved in the case have to say. Both the Law, and the Elders who administer that Law are called the "Kris", and this is a word which even the wildest of Gypsies fears.

The tribes' members often have well-known British names. Boswell, Buckland, Lee, Cooper, and Smith, are names given to large numbers of British Gypsies. The reason is that centuries ago they adopted the names of wealthy and influential men who had befriended them, or protected them against oppression. For much as a Gypsy appreciates freedom, he values protection also, and never resents a genuine "Gorgio" friend.

The tribes are also grouped in units named after the work they do, or that their forefathers did. There are the "Kalderash", meaning Coppersmiths, but including other Gypsies who work in metals. There are the "Gitanos" or Entertainers who include musicians and dancers of several kinds, and there are the "Manush" or Horse-people, who include circus hands and riders, as well as grooms, horse doctors and dealers.

The close links between families and these even larger groups, mean that Gypsies often cross the frontiers between different countries (usually by secret routes). For great events they will all gather at the same place, even though this means crossing much of Europe to get there.

When Gypsies travel, they usually do so in small groups, or even in single families. In this way they avoid attracting attention to themselves, while to strangers they may well deny that

Gypsies have their own system of law. They hold their courts, often in the open air, always in secret, and the decision of the "judges" who have been appointed by members of the tribe, is accepted as final. Women are not allowed to be present at these court hearings.

they have any knowledge of the presence of other Gypsies in the district.

But nevertheless, they are probably on their way to join them. They will do this by following the Sign Language, called by the Gypsies "Patrin", which tells them what direction other Gypsies have taken. Such signs are rarely noticed by ordinary passers by. For one thing, they are usually placed above the eye-level of a man on foot, but a gypsy holding the reins of his horse will be on the look-out from the high seat of his caravan, and will easily be guided by such insignificant things as a broken branch, a wisp of twisted straw, a few flowers which to others seemed to have been dropped quite aimlessly, and other minute signs which tell him all he needs to know.

Life has greatly changed for the Gypsy since the outbreak of the Second World War in 1939. Kept on the move, or else imprisoned by hostile and suspicious soldiers, the Gypsies had no documents, or ration books with which to obtain essential food.

They suffered greatly at the hands of the Nazis in Germany, who are alleged to have wiped out about 400,000 of Germany's pre-war Gypsy population. Even so, there are something between two and five million Gypsies still roaming the world today.

Though horse-drawn caravans may still be seen, many Gypsies – especially in England – have now changed the horse for the motor car. A powerful car pulls their modern-style caravan and, instead of dealing in horses, they deal in old cars, spare parts, and scrap metal.

Their 20th century caravan is far less picturesque than the old type, with its tall chimney, gay curtains, and painted wheels.

But their dumps of wrecked cars and rusty spares are less attractive to passers-by than were the well groomed horses of a former day.

With the demand for land to build new houses competing with the farmer's need for land for ploughing and grazing, and with the planning activities of Local Authorities, it is becoming more difficult than ever for Gypsies to find somewhere to camp. Local Councils are now required by law to provide sites where Gypsies may park their caravans for a limited time.

But tiresome rules and regulations are often forgotten by Gypsies, and many are the misunderstandings, insults, fights, and even "turnings-out" reported in local papers as carried out by Council officials supported by the police.

But when next you see a gypsy, remember that if he is a true "Rom", he has a wonderful history, a language and law of his own, and a whole way of life which it would be against his entire nature to give up or change, even in this modern age!

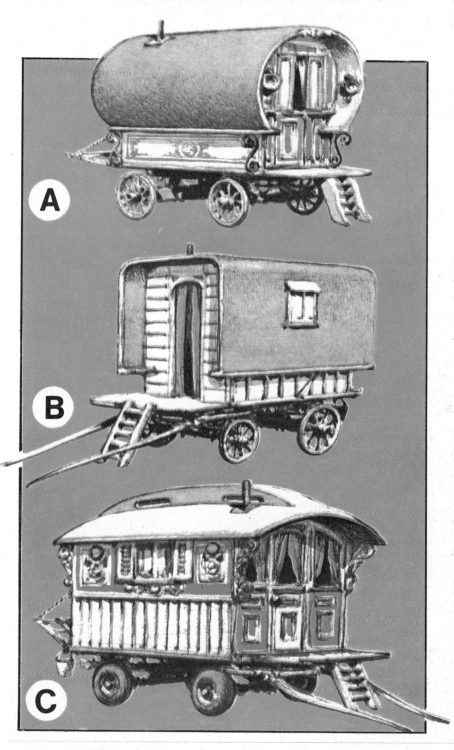

A true Gypsy calls his caravan or wagon a 'vardo'. Illustrated below are three types of Gypsy caravan. A. Barrel-topped wagon. B. Open Lot wagon. C. Skylight wagon.

Some of the special signs used by Gypsies when they are travelling about

Here they give nothing.

Beggars received badly.

Generous people.

Very generous people and friendly to Gypsies.

Here Gypsies are regarded as thieves.

Old woman died recently.

Old man died recently.

Marriage in the air.

THE FIGHTERS WHO KNEW NO FEAR

The Boxers were the most famous army of kung-fu fighters in history. They believed that nothing could harm them in their battles against their enemies.

A Boxer underwent a terrifying initiation test in which armed dummies slashed or stabbed at him with murderous ferocity.

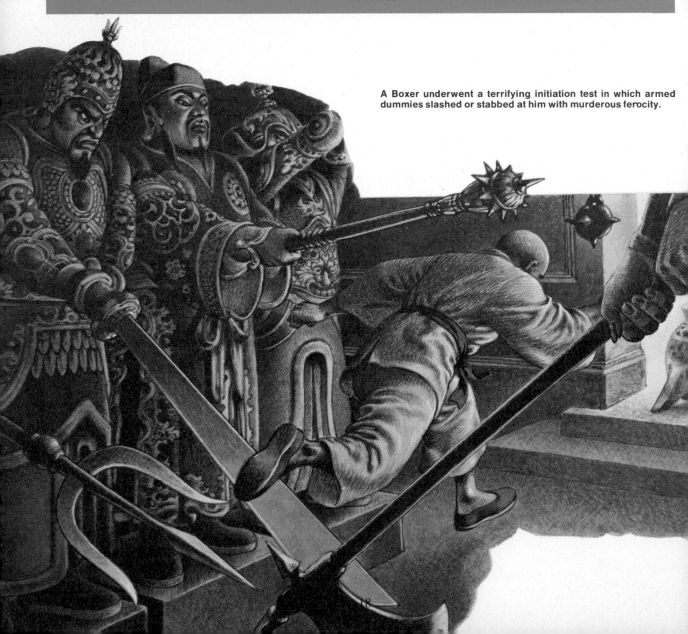

The Boxers were skilled, fearless and fanatical.

B ands of men could be seen carrying out a strange ritual all over the Shantung province of China in the year 1900. They were bowing, stamping and knocking their heads on the ground with their bodies facing the south-east.

Under the exhortation of their leader, these men would work themselves into a trance-like frenzy in which they believed they were immune to bullets or swords.

Finally, in their thousands, they would hurl themselves at the homes and offices of the Europeans living in Peking, determined at all costs to throw the "foreign devils" into the sea.

These were the *I Ho Chuan*, or "Fists of Righteous Harmony", better known as The Boxers, the most famous army of kung-fu fighters in history.

But although they were skilled, fearless and fanatical, the Boxers proved no match for Western fire power. Peking was besieged for 55 days, and when the city was finally relieved, the great mass of peasant-fighters melted away, leaving thousands of casualties behind them.

Puzzled and dismayed, they felt themselves betrayed by their leaders, who had sworn that nothing could harm them. What had gone wrong? The great kung-fu teachers of the past would have had a ready enough answer: the secrets of China's great martial art had been divulged to non-Buddhists and those who were not "gentle and merciful." And, of course, utter disaster had been the result.

Mysterious Origins

But how did such an apparently aggressive art come into the hands of Buddhist monks in the first place? And did it really originate with them, or was this deadly form of unarmed combat a skill that had been introduced into China from somewhere else? These are questions that are still argued about by experts even today. For, kung-fu is probably the great-grandfather of both karate and judo, and has its beginnings so far back in history that the truth about its origin has been lost.

In China, kung-fu is more generally known as *wu-schu*, or martial art. Kung-fu is not even directly translatable, although it describes a skill that in Hong Kong is called "War Art." Its name has been popularised in the West by the kung-fu films that were made in Hong Kong. Even thought this name may not be strictly accurate, it has become generally accepted throughout the rest of the world.

It is possible to trace what seem to be references to kung-fu as far back as 2,500 B.C. Certainly "boxing techniques" are mentioned in writings of about 600 B.C., although we do not know what kind of boxing this was. What is far more likely is that in about 500 A.D., a stranger arrived in China, bearing news of the form of Buddhism known as Zen. His name was Ta Mo, and, according to legend, he was the son of the Indian king, Sugandha. Given a chilly welcome by the emperor, Ta Mo settled in a monastery in the province of Honan, and after many years of silent meditation, began to teach.

Ta Mo's curriculum allowed little time for sleep, and it was not long before young monks began to show signs of exhaustion. One by one they collapsed, worn out by their master's harsh regime. Realising that the souls of his pupils could not benefit from his teaching if their bodies were weak, Ta Mo set about instructing them in a series of exercises that were to form the basis of kung-fu. Within a century, these were being followed throughout China.

So many stories of the origins of kung-fu stress

These kung-fu stances are called, from left to right: crane, cut and kneeling. The fifth position is the high kick.

ONLY FOR THE EXPERT!
Readers should not imitate any of these movements, except under skilled instruction.

its association with Buddhist monks, that one wonders why the followers of a religion of non-violence should wish to become expert in a martial art. Some kung-fu scholars believe that the monks learned self-defence as a mental and physical discipline, and also as a means of protecting themselves from marauders when they went on pilgrimages.

But there is another theory that makes a good deal of sense and provides a reason for the considerable secrecy that surrounded the masters of kung-fu.

When the Ming dynasty gave way to the rule of the Manchus, many former officials had to go into hiding. As the Manchus were superstitious, and generally avoided having anything to do with religious orders, the Ming officials disguised themselves as Buddhist monks and took refuge in a monastery. There they planned the revolution that would bring them back to power. According to legend, a monastery in Southern China housed two distinct sets of monks for many years. These were the genuine seekers after religious truth, and a group of political fanatics who spent their time making themselves as immune to harm as was humanly possible.

The passing out tests of these fanatics were formidable. Before they were allowed to set out and gather recruits to the Ming cause, they had to make their way through a temple filled with fiendishly ingenious wooden dummies. Each of these was equipped with some kind of lethal weapon. As the candidate walked through the temple, the pressure of his feet on the floor would activate one or more of the dummies, which would immediately slash or stab at him with murderous ferocity.

Should the man succeed in making his way between all the dummies, he would be faced with a final task. This consisted of making his way through a doorway in which stood a heavy metal jar that had been heated until it glowed red. The correct way for the student to remove the jar was to pick it up in his arms. This act branded him with two symbols engraved on the vessel, a dragon, and a tiger, which would remain with him for life as proof that he was master of kung-fu.

As with all the martial arts of the Orient, kung-fu relies heavily on mental training. Only with the aid of a completely disciplined mind can a student hope to gain control of his body. Consequently kung-fu training requires meditation and special exercises that may take years to master.

Animal Movements

Many martial art exercises are based on the movements of five animals – the bear, monkey, bird, tiger and deer. These were introduced by a famous doctor in about the year 200 A.D. Later, the properties of other creatures real and mythical, were added, not only to the exercises, but to the movements of kung-fu itself, so that there were the leopard movements, snake movements and even dragon movements.

Kung-fu reached the Western world in about the middle of the last century, when it appeared among the Chinese communities on the West coast of North America. Almost certainly it was taken there by the many Oriental workers who were employed on building the great, transcontinental railway systems. But, although it was more than a century old in our eyes, few people had heard of kung-fu until Bruce Lee appeared on the cinema screen, with his high kicking, hard hitting form of unarmed combat.

Kung-fu is very similar to karate. Indeed some say that it is only another name for Chinese karate. As a sport, it should only be followed under the guidance of a skilled instructor, and, unlike similar Japanese martial arts, it boasts no badges or belts to denote grades or proficiency, for to the true believer in kung-fu it is not a sport, but a way of life.

Self defence
techniques. Defence
against an attack with
a club. In these
pictures, the stick
represents a weapon.

How to ward off
a knife attack.

A 'punch' attack
and its defence.

The crane
stance and left
hand is being
used against a
kick, followed
by a blow to the
ribs.

A monument of ice that floats majestically upon the sea . . . a lake as big as Belgium . . . a mystifying labyrinth of underground caves. They are some of the most marvellous things on our planet. But you will not find them in the traditional list of the Seven Wonders of the World.

The reason for this is that they are among nature's seven wonders, and they are far more awe-inspiring than anything constructed by man.

Beside one of these wonders stands a monument to the man who discovered it. The man is David Livingstone, the missionary-explorer who, in 1852, set out on an expedition along the Zambesi River in Africa. By 3rd November, 1855, he had reached Linyati. As he journeyed, he noticed that the waters of the wide Zambesi were flowing faster. Soon, he was staring on the mighty falls to which he gave the name of his queen . . . the Victoria Falls.

Over a thousand metres deep and over one and a half kilometres wide, the river plunged down into a chasm that runs from east to west. Livingstone returned to the falls in 1860 and concluded that they were caused by a great fissure which had drained off the water of a great lake which he believed to have once occupied the centre of the continent.

Ask the Americans to name their country's greatest natural wonder and they will surely mention the Grand Canyon of the Colorado in northern Arizona. Discovered in 1540 by a Spaniard, Garcia Lopez de Cardenas, it is 330 km in length, from 12 to 32 km wide and has a depth of over 2,000 metres. It is considered the world's finest example of running water erosion.

Magnificent sights are plentiful, like the Fount of Hopi. This is an ancient spring through which the Hopi Indians believed their ancestors emerged from the underworld.

What gives the Grand Canyon its beauty are the walls of multi-coloured layers of rock, all varying in hue and representing an era in history. In them are fossils which show what animal and plant life was like in pre-history.

A party of explorers put another of America's natural wonders into the record books. Their expedition in 1972 proved that the Flint Ridge Caves in Kentucky were joined to the more famous Mammoth Cave system.

The entrance to the Flint Ridge Cave is through a magnificent cavern chamber called the Crystal Palace. On the Mammoth side is the Main Cave, whose rooms and passages extend for nearly five kilometres. In the Star Chamber, the roof of black manganese oxide sparkles with myriads of brilliant crystals. Another cave room of great beauty, the Bridal Altar Chamber, has the look of an ornate chapel.

Of all the world's wonders, none has presented more of a challenge to men than Mount Everest, which pierces the sky between Nepal and Tibet. Named after Sir George Everest, it is 8.85 km high, is permanently covered with snow and is difficult to climb. Many climbing expeditions tried in vain until the summit was scaled in 1953 by Sir Edmund Hillary of New Zealand and

The roaring waters of the Zambesi River cascade over the Victoria Falls.

WORLD

Sherpa Tenzing Norgay of Nepal. This was man's ninth attempt to get to the top of the world's highest mountain.

Mountains covered with trees arise on all sides of a fresh water lake bigger than Belgium. This is Lake Baikal in south-eastern Siberia. Around its shores is a mossy soil turned into a riot of colour by masses of wild flowers. This is the deepest lake in the world, having a depth of 1,940 metres. It is 620 km long and between 32 and 74 km wide.

One-fifth of the world's fresh water is in this lake. Living in it are 1,800 species of fish, plants and aquatic animals. Among them is a fish that is so transparent that you could almost read a book through it. This is the golomyanka.

There are seals, too, but how they found their way into the lake is a mystery, for they are normally salt water creatures. One theory is that, at an early stage of its existence, the lake

One of America's majestic beauty spots, the Grand Canyon, was discovered by a Spanish explorer in 1540.

Above: the Mammoth Cave system is part of an underground wonderland.

Right: Mount Everest – a towering challenge to mountaineers.

23

Lake Baikal in Siberia holds one-fifth of the world's fresh water.

must have been connected to the Arctic Ocean by a channel. It is presumed that the seals swam through this and bred in the lake, remaining there after geological changes had closed the channel.

Where do shimmering white mountains rise in perpendicular walls from the sea higher than anywhere else? There is only one answer to this question and that is Glacier Bay in Alaska. This bay is a frozen fairyland of sheer-walled glaciers on which the sunlight glistens.

In the bay are large chunks of floating ice. And here, too, are the fossilised trunks of trees that are supposed to have been growing before the pharaohs were building their pyramids in Egypt.

After they have taken shape slowly and grown constantly until they have become incredibly large, the glaciers slide into the sea, tearing the ground bare as they do so.

First and largest of America's great nature reserves is Yellowstone National Park which covers an enormous area in three states – Wyoming, Montana and Idaho.

When the Earth was young, volcanic fire ripped apart the globe's surface. Then came the Ice Age glaciers to mould it. The result is an incredible spectacle of mountains reaching to unimaginable heights, vast waterfalls crashing with thunderous roars into deep gorges, thousands of hot spring and thermal pools. Here, the water bubbles and steams into rock basins that glisten with colour like precious stones.

Above: one of the great nature reserves of America, Yellowstone National Park is well stocked with plant and wild life.

Left: Glacier Bay in Alaska is a fairyland of glistening ice.

CLOSE SHAVES

"Beaver!" Beastly little boys used to shout this at everything that moved in a beard. Then they would run off before the irate owners could assault them. This was standard practice in the 1920s, and as most of those then equipped with bristles were old men, they were unlikely to catch up with their tormentors.

How did the absence of beards come about? It was not simply a change in fashion, a deliberate desire to divest men's faces of anything remotely Victorian. It was really the doing of an American with a strange-sounding name, who was born in Wisconsin in 1855. He was called King Camp Gillette.

In those days anyone who could afford it was shaved daily by a barber, who was skilled in the use of the ominously nicknamed "cut-throat" razor. The rest of suffering male humanity struggled with their own cut-throats.

From the mid-18th century, a few public-spirited inventors added a guard to the cut-throat, most notably a Frenchman named Jean-Jacques Perret, but the sensible idea never caught on.

Came the 1890s and salvation for shavers, though not for barbers. They

Before Gillette came along with his safety razor, men had to use the ominously named "cut-throat" razor to rid their faces of unwanted hair.

were to be very annoyed at the loss of trade, caused by King Gillette, though, as we shall see, he had trouble getting his great idea turned into reality.

King Gillette never stopped thinking up ideas, while earning his living as a travelling salesman.

Then in 1895, just as he was starting to shave he found that his razor was blunt enough to need sharpening by a

specialist. It came to him in a flash that a razor was only a sharp edge and that everything behind that edge was just support. The backing was waste of labour and money: all that mattered was the edge. If that edge could be put on a piece of steel only thick enough to hold it . . . And at that moment the safety razor with its disposable blade was born.

But now the problem was how to make a blade sharp, thin, flat and cheap enough? He built a rough model straight away, but nobody believed in him, not merely the men with the money-bags who could have backed him, but even his friends, who cracked unfunny jokes every time they saw him. Not until 1901, six years after his brainwave, did he get financial backing. And then a young employee, named William Nickerson, invented machinery which made both razors and blades automatically. Yet in 1903, when it seemed that their fortunes were made, only 51 razors and 168 blades were sold.

Happily, word got around, and in 1904 sales spiralled to 90,844 razors and 123,648 blades, and figures after that became astronomical. And Gillette himself became world famous, for until the 1960s his face appeared on every packet of Gillette blades – and there were many millions of them.

Men who chose to wear beards often suffered the taunts of small boys.

BRITAIN'S ROYAL NAVY

1. The foundations of Britain's navy were set by Henry VIII, who formed the first central navy office. By Nelson's time, admirals were wearing their cocked hats "athwart" and sailors wore ribbons on their hats bearing the names of their ships.

2. In 1825, new regulations were made for Royal Naval uniforms. Ordinary sailors wore bell bottoms and simpler tunics. Officers wore peaked caps while at sea. Red collars and cuffs were introduced in 1830 when William IV came to the throne.

3. Red collars and cuffs for officers were done away with in 1843, and white was reintroduced. The new uniform regulations of 1856 introduced the curl on the top stripe for executive officers. The first official uniform for seamen appeared in 1857.

4. By the time the first ironclads appeared on the scene, seamen's dress had taken on a modern look. They wore blue shirts with their "bell bottoms". Coloured badges were also introduced to identify various branches.

5. A commander, a midshipman and an admiral of the 1870s. Officers' rank was now indicated by gold cuff bands, and peaked hats were more generally worn. The midshipman has white patches on his collar.

6. The Royal Navy played an important part in the "little wars" of the late nineteenth century. Small raiding parties of sailors fought in the Sudan and against the Boers. Our picture shows a petty officer ready to lead a raid.

7. The First World War saw the disappearance of many of the trimmings from naval uniforms. They became plainly functional and, except for the cut, were very similar to those worn today. After the outbreak of war, the marines ceased to wear red.

8. The Second World War brought more changes. Our picture shows a typical wartime sailor ready for action. Looking on are a Flag Captain (identified by the aigulette on his shoulder) and a Woman's Royal Naval Service officer in her tricorn hat.

9. Now today. A bandmaster of the Royal Marines adds a bright splash of colour as he speaks to an admiral of the fleet in full dress uniform. With them is a seaman in the uniform that is famous throughout the world.

26

'SACRIFICES MUST BE MADE'

These were the words of a man who made the supreme sacrifice attempting to prove that man could fly.

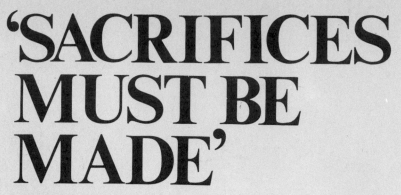

Otto Lilienthal.

"HOLD it Herr Lilienthal! Just one moment!" cried the photographer from beneath his voluminous black cloth. 15 metres above him a strange moth-like shape swung in the air.

"I am doing my best, mein herr," shouted its pilot. "but I don't rule the wind you know!" Even as Otto Lilienthal spoke, the breeze dropped and his flimsy glider soared away towards the foot of the hill.

"OK, I have the picture!" the photographer shouted in triumph — but nobody was listening. Otto Lilienthal was busy making a safe landing while the gaggle of journalists who had gathered to see some real flying were now rushing down the hill to interview the greatest man in the aviation world.

They reached Lilienthal as he was extricating himself from the glider. The year was 1895 and Lilienthal had proved that man could at least glide, even if nobody had as yet managed to build a flying machine with an engine.

"Herr — herr Lilienthal," said the first of the journalists to reach the glider. "Tell me about this wonderful machine of yours."

Otto Lilienthal smiled at his eager audience.

"This is my biplane, so called

As Lilienthal made a safe landing in his flimsy glider, the excited reporters rushed down the hill to interview the man who had proved at last that it was possible to fly.

Lilienthal spared no effort in his attempts to emulate the birds.

because it has two wings one above the other. I have given it the number 13. I have made three biplanes so far, with wing areas of 18, 10.5 and 20 square metres. They are very stable, which came as a surprise to me, and I have flown in winds of about 25 mph, as you yourselves saw. Ah, here comes our photographer! I hope your picture is a success mein herr. As I was saying, when the wind is strong my glider seems to remain stationary. But there are many more problems to solve."

Otto Lilienthal was a quiet and rather humble man, though he was ever eager to spread his discoveries around and perhaps encourage other people to experiment. Many men before him had tried to fly. Many had died or at least suffered injury, but Otto Lilienthal was a new type of "aeronaut". He approached the subject carefully and slowly with a scientific mind, though this care in no way dampened his fanatical determination to fly.

Ever since he had been a boy back in the 1850's Otto Lilienthal had longed to fly. He and his brother even made a six wing ornithopter which was supposed to fly by flapping its wings like a bird. It failed, but right up to his death Lilienthal believed he could build a flying machine that would flap its way into the air. Fortunately for himself, and for the science of aviation, Otto decided to learn as much about flying by gliding as he could.

Like so many advances in science flying didn't happen suddenly on its own. Many dedicated would-be aviators had tried to build flying machines but had always failed. They had tried studying the birds, but had quickly found that their wing movements were too fast to be observed accurately. But then came the camera. By halting motion on a photographic plate the workings of a bird's wing could be studied in detail.

Even so, study on the ground was not good enough – not for a man like Lilienthal.

"The manner in which we have to meet the irregularities of the wind," he once wrote, "can only be learned by being in the air itself."

Early Failures

So Otto Lilienthal studied, wrote, built and flew. To start with he had his failures just like everyone else. Lilienthal's Glider No. 1 had no tail and not surprisingly failed to fly. Glider No. 2 did have a tail but still wouldn't fly. Lilienthal first tried to get into the air by jumping off a springboard, then he tried running down hills into the wind. With Glider No. 3 Otto Lilienthal at last got off the ground – but only briefly.

No. 3 was built in 1891. It had a fixed tail and fin. From this moment on nothing could stop Otto Lilienthal. His boyhood dreams were nearing success. More gliders followed.

Lilienthal even had a high artificial hill thrown up near a brickworks in Lichterfelde, a suburb of Berlin. On top of this conical mound was a conical hanger in which the gliders were stored. From here Otto could launch himself in any direction he wished depending on where the wind was coming from. In that same year of 1894 Lilienthal built Glider No. 9. It was a monoplane like all his early gliders but this time the German aviator fixed a horizontal bow of willow in front of the wing as a shock absorber. As he crashed, it was just as well that he did.

In 1895 Otto Lilienthal built his first biplane glider, but by now his luck was running out. Lilienthal himself said "sacrifices must be made", but still he went on experimenting, improving and building up impressive hours of flying time.

News of his exploits, and photographs of him actually in the air, spread across the world inspiring others to build flying machines.

Lilienthal's gliders had made him famous, but in the end they killed him. On a bright sunny day in August 1896 Otto Lilienthal was gliding in a standard No. 11 type monoplane. People watched in admiration, then to their horror they felt a sudden gust of wind. Lilienthal's glider stopped in mid-air. They saw him throw himself forward to try and get the nose down – but it was too late. The glider stalled, its wing dropped and the No. 11 type side-slipped into the ground.

At first it looked like a minor smash for the glider was only damaged on one wing, but Otto Lilienthal lay unconscious some way away, having been thrown from the wreck. He felt no pain, but his back was broken. Next day in the Bergmann Clinic in Berlin Lilienthal died. On his gravestone they carved the motto "Opfer Müssen gebracht werden – Sacrifices must be made", Otto Lilienthal's own words.

PAXTON'S PALACE

The Victorians, outwardly at least so prim and proper, did not believe in exhibiting themselves in any shape or form. They had heard vaguely of the curious affairs across the Channel, where in Paris the French had put on no less than a dozen international exhibitions in the first half of the 19th century.

But it was not the way British people went about things . . . and therefore when, in 1849, the idea was put forward that all the nations of the world should be invited to take part in a vast exhibition in London, there were considerable misgivings.

As it happened, the inspiration came from no less a personage than Prince Albert himself. Queen Victoria's beloved husband envisaged an exhibition that would demonstrate the "development of mankind and the unity of the nations."

The very thought of London being invaded by thousands of foreigners horrified many of his subjects, and when the Prince further suggested that the exhibition should be sited in Hyde Park, the fears and the indignation knew no bounds.

Doctors feared the plague; manufacturers said the country would be flooded by cheap products; members of Parliament warned that cut-throats and anarchists would cause havoc in the capital of the Empire; and the lives of all would be endangered.

Then Joseph Paxton, formerly head gardener to the Duke of Devonshire, who had already put up a huge glass conservatory at Chatsworth, submitted his design to the Exhibition Commissioners. *The Times* newspaper described it scathingly as "a monstrous greenhouse"; but the public, when they saw the sketches published, were enthusiastic, and work began on the construction of the Crystal Palace.

The amount of glass required in the building of the Palace consumed one-third of the nation's output for a year.

Construction work began in August 1850, as 2,000 workmen swarmed around the Hyde Park site.

In an astonishing 17 weeks the "greenhouse" was completed. On 1st May, 1851, the Great Exhibition was opened by Queen Victoria and Prince Albert. All night long, enormous crowds, who had come in from the provinces, camped out in London.

At least 700,000 spectators lined the route as the Royal Family drove from Buckingham Palace to Hyde Park, and 25,000 were crammed inside the main transept as, to a flourish of trumpets, the exhibition was declared open.

Beneath the flags of forty different nations fluttering over the Crystal Palace, there were £2 million worth of exhibits, ranging from chairs made out of coal to the latest wonder, patent trousers without braces.

Amid the palms, the tropical foliage, the flowers and the fountains both the useful and the useless were exposed to the view of thousands of visitors strolling among the exhibits.

Certainly all the gloomy prophecies which had greeted the plans for the

exhibition were unfulfilled. None of the foreigners who flooded into London attempted to overthrow the monarchy, and apart from an influx of pick-pockets, there was no increase in crime.

When, on 15th October, 1851, the Great Exhibition finally closed, over six million visitors had passed through the Crystal Palace, and a delighted Queen Victoria bestowed a knighthood on its designer, Joseph Paxton.

Better still, the commissioners were able to announce that the exhibition had made a profit of £186,000, with which 70 acres of land was developed in South Kensington to found such great institutions as the Imperial College of Science and the Museums of Natural History, Science, Geology and, of course, the Victoria and Albert.

In 1852, the Crystal Palace was moved, lock, stock and barrel, to a new site in Sydenham, South London, where it served as a concert and recreation centre for millions of Londoners. In 1936, however, it was totally destroyed in a blaze that could be seen from fifty miles away.

But the museums of Kensington remain as solid witnesses to the success of the Great Exhibition.

NATURALLY NOSY

Whether scurring over the ground in short bursts waving its bushy tail like a banner, or sitting on a branch holding a nut in its forepaws, with its tail arched over its back, it is difficult not to like the grey squirrel. It is therefore unfortunate that these entertaining little acrobats should also be serious pests.

By eating the growing tips, or stripping the bark, they cause stunted and deformed growth in trees and are regarded as a major enemy by foresters.

In the garden, where grey squirrels are increasingly common as residents, they are inquisitive opportunists permitting little to escape their attention. They will quickly become fearless visitors to the bird table and in between times create mayham in the vegetable plot.

Although mainly vegetarian, squirrels will eat birds eggs (including those of domestic hens) and nestlings, there is however, reason to believe that this is less common than has been suggested.

Natives of North America grey squirrels were first introduced into this country, as a novelty, in about 1876. Currently, and in spite of repeated attempts at their extermination, they have spread over most of England and Wales and are slowly moving northwards through Scotland.

At Home In A Hole

The squirrels nest, called a drey, is built in the branches of a tree, it is a bulky structure of leafy twigs with a domed roof and is lined with leaves, dried grasses and moss. Occasionally natural holes in trees, enlarged if necessary, are used.

Squirrels do not hibernate, although being particularly susceptible to chills resulting from becoming wet, they seldom venture outside their dreys during inclement weather. In very cold spells several squirrels will sometimes share a drey for common warmth.

Breeding can start as early as the end of December and last until June. The young, usually three, but up to seven, are born naked and blind. Their eyes open in about three weeks, weaning takes between seven and ten weeks and they are sexually mature in six to ten months.

The grey squirrel is often blamed for the dwindling numbers of our native red squirrel, but the later was already in decline, possibly from changes in habitat, before the grey was introduced.

MAKING A MEAL

More than oil is coming from the wells beneath the North Sea and in the Middle East. Food, too, is coming from these subterranean store-houses of nature's wealth. For proteins, produced from paraffin or gas oil, could prove to be the solution to a growing world-wide problem.

This is caused by the fact that a large segment of mankind is suffering from protein-deficient diets, and traditional methods of producing food are falling behind rather than catching up with protein demand. For example, estimates point to a world-wide protein shortage of the order of 20 million tons a year by 2000.

One of the leaders in preventing a diet disaster is the British oil concern, BP, which has developed a method of producing yeast from oil. The result is a substance named Toprina which is being used in animal feeds, thus freeing supplies of traditional protein sources such as soya bean and fish meal for human consumption. Assuming public acceptance, the company hopes that its yeast will eventually be used as food for people.

Food For Animals

Yeasts have been used by man from very early times, primarily in the production of alcoholic drinks and in bread-making. More recently, a major use has been in the formulation of animal feeds.

Today, however, it is acknowledged that there is a general shortage of protein in

34

OF OIL

North Sea Oil—the solution to a food shortage?

the diet of a large part of the world's human population. Reputable authorities have said that some two-thirds of the present population has a protein intake well below their needs.

With a forecast of a world population of six billion by the year 2000, one can foresee only a worsening situation unless a source of supply immune from the vagaries of nature can be tapped. One such source is oil.

Proteins are essential constituents of every living organism. With the exception of fat, all tissues in our bodies are composed of proteins of one sort or another. The chemical reactions in the body by which we breathe, eat and move are controlled by enzymes and hormones which are themselves constructed from protein molecules.

World-wide, their primary source is plant life which uses carbon dioxide in the air and sunlight to produce organic material including proteins. They are very complicated substances containing carbon, hydrogen, oxygen and nitrogen, and most contain sulphur.

Proteins are, themselves, made of much simpler compounds known as amino acids of which 22 are normally found in proteins from natural sources. Simple-stomached animals, including man, are unable to synthesise some of the amino acids they require and so these—the so-called essential amino acids—have to be supplied in their diets.

Unfortunately, proteins of the most common vegetables lack

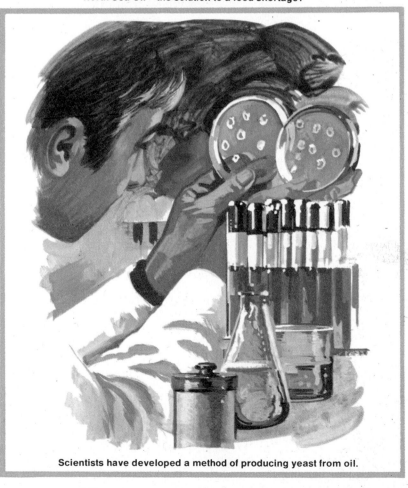

Scientists have developed a method of producing yeast from oil.

some of these essential building blocks, particularly lysine. Consequently, animal proteins are man's most important means of maintaining a balanced diet as they contain a full range of amino acids.

Raising animals is often a more expensive way of producing food than crops. It takes seven calories of plant carbohydrate to produce one calorie of beef protein.

The provision of food for the animals—and consequently for Man—is vital. How more of this could be provided was presenting agriculturalists with a headache until, in 1959, a French research team under Alfred Champagnat discovered that yeast micro-organisms grew well on the waxy normal paraffins in gas oil.

As work progressed on this, another yeast-producing project was set up in Scotland at Grangemouth. By 1965, two pilot plants were in operation—in France and Scotland— producing yeast which was

extensively tested for toxicity and nutritional value.

The standards applied were as vigorous as any yet devised for a feedstuff. And the result was a clean bill of health for the yeast which was permitted for use in nine countries.

Two processes are in use for the manufacture of these proteins. One is called The Normal Paraffin Process and the other is The Gas Oil Process.

The first method starts with the introduction of n-paraffins and other feed materials including mineral nutrients (potassium, magnesium, sulphate and phosphate), air, ammonia and water. These go into a fermenter where any micro-organisms present are killed by heat-treatment.

Major Component

Air at a controlled rate and gaseous ammonia enter through a sterilising filter. Mechanical agitation mixes the ingredients.

Animal feed extracted from oil has proved highly successful with poultry.

The desired strain of yeast is then injected into the chamber and begins growing and continues at a rate that produces one ton of yeast for every ton of feed stock. The mineral nutrients are taken up by the organisms.

The yeast then goes through processes which dry it and convert it into a powder which can be easily packed and transported.

In the gas-oil process, the operation is similar to the paraffin method, but there is no sterilisation before fermentation. Fermentation takes place in large vessels open to the atmosphere. Air is bubbled through the mixture at a high rate.

Various processes remove the gas oil and water from the mixture leaving the yeast in the form of a cream which is dried by being sprayed into a heated chamber and then stored for future use.

Trials started in October, 1965, on the use of yeasts produced in this way as part of the diet of pigs and poultry. These animals were chosen because of their requirement for high-quality protein.

Later, work was extended to cover young calves and baby lambs. These tests have showed that the yeasts are safe and valuable components of animal feeds.

Fast Grower

Fishmeal, with its high protein content and well balanced amino acid pattern, has always been regarded as the most valuable conventional protein source. It is the standard against which all other materials are compared. Together with soya bean meal, it forms the major protein component of the high nutrient feeds for pigs and poultry.

Yeast produced by the processes described here has proved its value as a partial or total replacement for fish and soya bean meals. And it has served as a partial skimmed milk replacement for calves.

Guaranteed to be regular in supply, independent of climatic conditions, yeasts grown on oil could help to save the world from starvation in the not too distant future.

THE WRIGHTS PROVED THEM WRONG

The Wright brothers tossed a coin to see which would make the first attempt to become airborne in the *Flyer*.

It all depended on the toss of a coin.

Who would be the first man to fly . . .?

Wilbur, the elder of the two brothers, won the toss and crawled carefully on to the lower wing of their *Flyer*.

The *Flyer*, a flimsy construction of struts and fabric, was the result of seven years' hard study, research and work. For Wilbur and Orville Wright were not the kind of men who stuck together a crack-pot contraption in the hope that it might work. Everything about their aeroplane was the outcome of experiment, testing and careful scientific observation.

The Wrights were determined young men who lived in Dayton, in Ohio, where their father was bishop of a local church. They had begun their working lives selling bicycles. Later on they built the bicycles they sold, and were successful enough in business to have the money available for their flying experiments.

They studied the wing motions of gliding birds. They spent many hours observing the local buzzards, and noticed how the birds kept themselves level in the air by twisting the ends of their wings.

When they built their first aircraft, a 1.5 metre wide kite in August 1899, the Wrights remembered the buzzards and arranged the wings so that they could be bent and twisted like the buzzards' wings. This technique became known as wing-warping and was used to great effect by the Wright brothers. In modern aircraft ailerons have taken the place of wing-warping. This bi-plane kite was an experimental model, controlled by wires from the ground, and the brothers used this to test out several of their early ideas.

The next step was to build themselves a full-sized glider. This they completed in September the following year. It already had the basic shape that they were to use for many years to come. It was a bi-plane with squarish wings and the elevator (a small "wing" for steering the aircraft up or down) to the front. A few gliding flights were made in this, but again it was flown mainly as a kite, so that the brothers could test out their theories without risk.

Two more gliders followed, each an improvement on the former.

When satisfied that they had solved the basic problems of keeping an aircraft in the air, and of being able to control it reasonably well, the brothers were then faced with the problem of power and propulsion. Since there were no small engines light enough and powerful enough to be of use in their aeroplane they built one themselves.

It drove two propellors, which they had designed and made entirely by themselves. Bicycle chains were used from the engine to the propellers, which rotated in opposite directions to keep the aircraft in balance.

The propellers were of the "pusher" type and mounted behind the wings. Thus with the propellers at the rear and the elevator "tail" in the front the Wrights' *Flyer* has a strange back-to-front appearance.

At long last, all was made ready for the first historic flight of mankind. The date was Monday, 14th December, 1903. The place was some sand dunes at Kill Devil Hills about 6 kilometres from Kitty Hawk.

At a signal the aircraft was unleashed.

The *Flyer* lurched forwards, gathering speed rapidly. It lifted slightly. Orville watched his brother, a black blob in a quivering web of wire and tubing.

The contraption parted from the wooden ramp. Wilbur moved the elevator control. In modern terms, he over-corrected and the *Flyer* obstinately dipped its nose into the Kill Devil sand. The flight had ended before it had begun.

Orville and the little band of helpers ran up. Wilbur was unhurt, but he had not become the first man in history to fly. There could be no more attempts that day because the *Flyer* had been slightly damaged. History would have to wait for the repairs to be done.

On the dull morning of Thursday, 17th December, 1903, the *Flyer* was again ready to make history.

This time it was brother Orville Wright's turn at the controls. He lay flat on one of the lower wings, slightly off-centre to balance the weight of the engine beside him. Just after half past ten the engine was started and the long, fragile-looking wings of the aircraft were held steady as the engine warmed and the twin propellers bit at the chill air. A stiff wind blew into the men's faces. On the dunes of Kill Devil Hills this steady wind could be relied upon. This was an important factor.

Wilbur gave the signal for the flight to begin. The lines holding back the aircraft were let go. The *Flyer*, powered by its noisy 12 hp engine began to move smoothly forwards. Its landing skids were resting on a two wheeled frame which ran along a wooden mono-rail some 18.2 metres long to ensure it had a friction-free take-off run.

After some nervous seconds the aircraft rose off its wheeled yoke. It was flying . . . actually flying!

Wilbur ran after the machine in his excitement. The five local people who had been persuaded to come along as witnesses of this historic event watched the scene from their coat-collars, hunched against the morning cold. Someone took a photograph, all unaware that this was to be the only pictorial record of one of the most stupendous events in the history of man.

Each brother made two flights that morning. Wilbur making the last and the longest at noon, remaining in the air for 59 seconds.

Needless to say, the determined cycle-makers did not finish with their aeroplanes with this success, tremendous though it was. They immediately began work on a *Flyer II*, and nine months later had flown the first aerial circuit. The *Flyer III*, in which Wilbur toured Europe in 1908, remained airborne for a sensational hour and a half . . . or approximately the time a manned satellite takes to orbit the earth.

After some seconds the aircraft rose off its wheeled yoke. It was flying . . . actually flying!

One of the many islands close to Venice, San Giogio Maggiore. Tourists enjoy the view of Venice from the tall bell tower (campanile).

Where The Highways Are Waterways

Boats take the place of cars and lorries. This powerful speedboat is an ambulance.

Venice is built on 118 islands, linked by over 400 footbridges. If you want to travel in Venice you must either walk, or go by boat.

The first people to live where Venice now stands wanted to escape from enemies on the mainland. They drove great wooden tree-trunks into the ground to add strength to the islands. Over the centuries they became rich and powerful by trading with many countries.

In 1966 waves 3.6 metres high rushed into the city, damaging buildings and destroying priceless works of art. Helpers have come from all over the world to restore the famous city. Unfortunately Venice is slowly sinking. The heavy marble and brick buildings still rely on the original wooden foundations. Scientists and engineers are seeking ways in which to stop the city from disappearing beneath the sea.

Normally Venice and nearby islands are protected from the Adriatic Sea by a long strip of land, but occasionally high tides and strong winds threaten the very existence of this unique and beautiful city which has already survived over 1,000 years.

Although there are no roads through Venice, the boats on the waterways still have to obey traffic signs, like the No-Entry warning on the bridge (top left).

Above: even the post goes by boat.

Left: St Mark's Basilica. The use of rare marbles, mosaics and golden decorations make this one of the world's most beautiful buildings.

Below: The Grand Canal is over 3 kilometres long and up to 70 metres wide, but little more than 5 metres deep. It passes 200 palaces and churches, some over 500 years old.

THE COUSIN OF THE CROW

The Common Magpie *(Pica pica)* is a very striking bird in its appearance. Its back, wings, tail, breast and head are black with a superb green-purple gloss. This contrasts with the otherwise white plumage and the white bar across its tail. Adult magpies of this species measure approximately 45 centimetres in length.

Magpies are generally found in pairs and seldom nest in large groups, although large numbers of pairs may be seen flocking after the breeding season during the autumn or early winter. They often build several nests, but only one of these is used. Usually in April, the female lays between 5-8 eggs and the incubation takes about 8 days. Like most of the crow family, the fledgeling period (when the young leave the nest) is about 2-3 weeks.

The Corvidae (the scientific name for the crow family) are generally accepted as being the most intelligent of all the bird families. This is indicated by the large numbers of crows and their close relatives that have been kept in captivity. They are easily taught tricks and their powers of mimicry are often amazing.

Not To Be Seen

There are at least 100 species of crow distributed throughout most of the world, though they are more prominent in the Northern Hemisphere and entirely absent from the Antarctic and certain other places such as New Zealand.

Generally, crows are considered quite large birds which inhabit forests, woods and brushland but, due to their habit of eating almost anything, they have become fairly familiar in towns and villages. Some of them have even learned to look for scraps of waste products from food processing factories, often competing with gulls for the privilege of sorting out the food from local corporation waste tips.

In spite of their powers of mimicry, crows are not considered to have a pleasant song voice. Most of them make a coarse, raucous sound quite unlike the flute-like noise of their close relative, the Oriole. Their beaks are strong and heavy, and often the nostrils are covered with forward pointing bristles, the exact function of which is not known, but there are a number of theories. One of these is that the bristles act as a sort of filter in a similar way to the hairs in our own nostrils.

Young magpies leave the nest when they are ▶ between

Keeping An Eye On The Weather

The collecting of weather data is probably the world's most widespread industry. There are at least 7,000 land-based stations scattered across the islands and continents, each with its barometers, thermometers, sunshine recorders and other instruments.

The standard equipment varies, but a fully instrumented station makes more than 20 kinds of observations, while all stations send in reports at six hourly intervals to their local centres.

At sea, data from weather ships is supplemented by thousands of reports from cargo and passenger craft. Airliners radio in their observations, as do the patrolling military flights. Radar scanners examine the structure of the rainclouds and measure the diameter of the drops they contain.

Valuable as the land and sea observations are, it is in the upper levels of the atmosphere that the main forces controlling the weather are to be found. Extensive explorations of this region are made with balloons, aircraft, rockets and satellites.

Every day, hundreds of balloons shoot skywards, trailing parachutes and packages of instruments. Readings from these are transmitted as musical notes, which the receiving stations converts into understandable information.

At roughly 20,000 metres, as the surrounding air pressure drops, the balloons expand and burst, parachuting their packages back to Earth. While in the air, they transmit information about air and humidity to ground stations. By tracing the balloon with radar, the weathermen can determine wind direction and speed.

The data produced by all of these methods is not only of value to pilots, farmers and others who need an accurate forecast. In areas where hurricanes, monsoon floods or high seas are a danger, early weather warnings will even save lives.

Seeding has been used to take the sting out of a hurricane. Rockets carrying silver iodide particles are fired at the turbulent clouds which surround it. This produces freezing which causes the release of a tremendous amount of heat. This heat disrupts the wall of the hurricane's eye, causing it to rebuild outwards. This extending of the wall slows the furious winds.

The tornado is not so easy to detect in advance as a hurricane. Space weather satellites cannot see the build-up of a tornado. All they can make out are the storms which are most likely to give birth to one. Scientists are hoping one day to be able to devise ways of reducing the ferocity of tornadoes that every year destroy homes, take lives and cause millions of pounds worth of damage in the United States.

The possibility of deliberately controlling the weather has been explored by man for centuries. As scientific knowledge has increased, he has built huge fires to see if he can create clouds, fired cannons to turn moisture in the atmosphere to rain and, more recently, hurled rockets into thunderstorms in the hope of reducing the damaging effects of hail.

To some extent, weather has been modified. A good example is the use of heaters and fans in fruit orchards to prevent frost damage to the crops. And during World War Two fog over airfields was dissipated – at great expense – by burning petrol beside the runways.

Before we can fully control the weather, we need to know much more about natural clouds and the causes of rainfall. We have to find out how storms develop, how lightning is created, how rain is produced and how hurricanes and tornadoes grow. When man has solved these problems, he will be able to create the climate he desires – and make weather forecasting an interesting, but obsolete, science.

Was Stonehenge once a sanctuary for Stone Age man?

Strange Secret Of The Stone Circle

Stonehenge is situated on Salisbury Plain in Wiltshire. It is one of the most popular tourist attractions in Britain. Below; the massive stone circle as it must have looked when it was first built.

Who laboured with huge stones over vast distances to set those stones upright on a wild plain in Wiltshire? Two miles from Amesbury, these stones, many of them still standing, are left as a remembrance of a very ancient people who made upon this place a "Henge", or sanctuary. A sanctuary from what, and to whom?

Stonehenge was ancient when first the Romans marched by it. There the soldiers rested a while to eat. We know this, for they left pottery fragments and bones. Years later, when Rome had made all England her own, did her people come to Stonehenge and stare at the great stones with amazement and wonder?

Centuries later, the Saxons also rested awhile at Stonehenge. They, too, left pieces of pottery and meat bones. Perhaps they pitched their tents against the mighty stones, for the Saxons feared the Roman towns. They left them to rot and weather away. But Stonehenge was so ancient that it clearly held no ghosts for these invaders.

Over the years, treasure-hunters have dug beneath the stones, and found no treasure. Some of the stones were removed for building material. Others fell and broke, and all are weathered by thousands of years of wind, sun and rain. Yet enough stones are left standing for men of all ages to wonder—wonder—who were the people who set them up, and why?

In the 14th century it was thought that Merlin, the magician of King Arthur's tales, was responsible for the Giants' Dance as Stonehenge was then called. From an old manuscript we read: "... Merlin brought the Giants" Dance by art, not by force, from Ireland to England.'

Sacrificial Stone

Later it was believed that the site was a Druids' Temple, and that human sacrifices took place on Midsummer Day and upon a stone which is now called the Slaughter Stone.

But modern knowledge of archaeology tells us that this Stonehenge, or sanctuary, was set up long, long before the Druids came with the Iron Age Celts.

We know now that Stonehenge was started by Stone Age man in the Neolithic Age – that is the New Stone Age, some 1,800 years before Christ was born. It was made and re-made many times, and completed about 1,400 B.C. By then ancient man was using bronze, so that the final Stonehenge is a Bronze Age sanctuary – the finest of its time and kind in the whole of Europe.

For many years, almost as a

How could early man have transported such huge blocks of stone such as those used in the construction of Stonehenge? One theory is that logs were used as rollers, enabling the stones to be hauled across the rough countryside by gangs of men.

We do not know exactly how Stonehenge was built but one theory is illustrated below. First, a sloping bank of earth was built up to form a ramp. A big stone was then pushed over the top of the ramp and slid down into a hole dug in the ground.

When two upright stones were in position the earth was built up to the top of them. A smaller stone was dragged up the bank and placed across them. Then the earth was dug away leaving the stones in position.

legend, it was thought that the Bluestones came from Wales. This has now been proved. The stones known as Spotted Dolerite came from the Prescelly Hills in Pembrokeshire. The so-called Sarsen stones have been found to come from the Marlborough Downs.

There are many theories, none of them proved, as to how those very early men brought the Bluestones from Wales. One belief is that they came overland, crossing the River Severn at a point higher up than Gloucester. Another theory has it that they came by sea, round Land's End to the mouth of the Hampshire Avon and up the river.

The Sarsen stones would have to come by overland route. They could have been lashed on to rough sledges, made from whole tree-trunks. When the ground was hard with frost and ice, they could have been dragged. Their sheer weight would have bogged them down in soft or marshy ground.

It is thought that these great Sarsen stones were erected after the Bluestones. In fact, the Bluestones were taken down and the site levelled for the Sarsen stones to be erected. Later, the Bluestones were set up in new positions.

The shape of Stonehenge is circular with a horse-shoe shape within it. An avenue leads up to the Henge, with an earth mound around the standing stones, and a ditch beyond.

Standing Stones

Using only stones as tools, those early men made dowels and dowel-holes in the Sarsen stones, and so erected so-called Trithons – that is to say two standing stones with a lintel across them to form a shape like that of a doorway, or open window. Also with "hammerstones" they dressed – or smoothed – certain sides of the stones. All these dressed sides are facing inwards, and the irregular, rough sides outwards. With the

hammerstones pounding away at the huge blocks, curves could be straightened out.

The Sarsen stones seem to have arrived groomed and ready for erection. The Bluestones, on the other hand, seem to have been dressed at the same time that the Sarsens were put in place. These must have been very rough when first erected.

But why did these early men work so hard to leave this mark of their existence? Was it started to the memory of some great chieftain? Who knows? All around the countryside are the burial places of early man, the long barrows, and later the round barrows. As Stonehenge stands now there is no great burial chamber. Could there once have been?

Was Stonehenge a tribal meeting place, or a place of worship? It was, as we know, often remodelled, so that it must have been used over hundreds of years.

Sun-stone

In 1771, a Dr. John Smith pointed out that upon the longest day the sun rose first above the stone now called the Heel-stone, or the Sun-stone. This is a large, undressed standing-stone with a naturally pointed top. Today, with very careful observation, we find that the first sunrays at the Summer Solstice – that is the longest day – shine just a little to the left of the peak. When Stonehenge was built the sun would have risen *exactly* above this pointed stone.

Over the years it has been worked out that the rising and the setting of the sun over certain stones clearly make of Stonehenge a standing calendar. And those early men must have worked *that* out!

If you stand in the centre of Stonehenge on the shortest day – the Winter Solstice – the sun sets through one of the great doorways of a Trithon, with two great Trithons upon either side.

TALE OF A TAIL

The long-tailed field or wood-mouse is a gentle attractive little creature with a long tapering tail that accounts for almost half its total length of about 180 mm.

Although it can sometimes be seen feeding during the day, it is, as its large black eyes suggest, mainly nocturnal in its habits and when not searching for food, it spends most of its time below ground where it makes extensive tunnels. It prefers dry woodland or hedgerows with plenty of ground cover, but it can often be seen in gardens. During the winter months it will sometimes venture indoors.

The long-tailed mouse is omnivorous, that is it feeds on both plant and animal food and it is certainly not fussy. Berries, roots, seeds, fruit, nuts, insects and the bodies of other mice or birds, all form part of its diet. In the garden it is particularly partial to peas and beans, and will energetically dig for crocus and daffodil bulbs.

Raider

It has been seen raiding beehives, in search of honey, and salmon hatcheries, for eggs.

The long-tailed field mouse is the prey of many creatures – stoats, weasels, foxes, tawny owls, barn owls, kestrels, and of course the domestic cat.

It usually relies on it's speed and tremendous jumping ability to escape, but in common with the dormouse and yellow-necked mouse, it has an interesting additional defence mechanism – a disposable tail. If its tail is grasped, the skin just slides off leaving behind the naked vertebrae which after a few days fall off to leave a small permanent stump.

The courtship of long-tailed mice is vigorous and their breeding prolific. In a season lasting from March to October, or longer in a mild winter, five or more litters are produced. The mother usually becomes pregnant again immediately after giving birth.

From two to nine young are born in the nest which is constructed of finely chopped grass and is situated at the end of a short burrow or in the roots of a tree. Blind at birth, their eyes open in 12 to 14 days and they are weaned and independant in about three weeks.

Since the young are sexually mature at seven to eight weeks those born early in the year can themselves breed before the season ends.

WHEN SINBAD SAILED THE SEAS

Sindbad of Baghdad, better known as Sindbad the Sailor, was piloting a ship from southern India to South Arabia across the Indian Ocean.

"Which port are you heading for?" the ship's captain asked him.

"Raysut, or a mile north or south of it," was Sindbad's reply.

"You will miss it by at least fifty miles!" the captain declared, but Sindbad was confident of his navigation and simply smiled. So the two voyagers made a bet for twenty gold coins.

Fifteen days later, after sailing 1500 miles across the open ocean without a sight of land and of course in those days without a compass or a ship's clock, they saw a mountain. The following morning, before dawn, Sindbad ordered the crew to drop anchor. Then he turned to the captain and asked him where they were.

"About fifty miles from Raysut."

"No, we are at Raysut itself, or a bow-shot on either side of it," Sindbad replied confidently. Slowly the sun rose behind them and, pink in the light of dawn, the tall houses of Raysut came into view. Sindbad won his bet and like a good Muslim gave his profits to the poor.

Of course Sindbad the Sailor is simply a character from the Arabian Nights fairy-tales — but change that name to Muhammad ibn Babishad and this story becomes true. The voyage was made around AD 930 by an Arab merchant ship returning home, perhaps laden with silks and eastern spices, from Fansur in what is now Indonesia.

While the Vikings of the north were making their voyages of discovery and conquest in sleek longships, the Arabs of the south were making even longer journeys on a much more regular and peaceful basis throughout much of the typhoon tossed Indian Ocean.

Their ships were the direct ancestors of those Arab dhows that still sail today. They were quite unlike the ships of the medieval Mediterranean, for their planks were sown rather than nailed together. They were made from teak or coconut-palm wood, and above all they had triangular lateen sails like those used aboard modern racing yachts. These more advanced sails enabled Arab mariners to tack into the wind, which even the Vikings could not do effectively in their square-rigged ships.

The seasonal monsoons of the Indian Ocean were also a bonus, for these regular and predictable winds helped Arab sailors make annual voyages directly across the open sea at a time when Europeans — even Vikings — did all they could to avoid losing sight of land. The Greeks supposedly "discovered" these monsoons in the 1st century AD though of course local sailors had known about them for years.

Even before the creation of the huge Muslim Empire in the 7th century AD, sea-borne trade in the Indian Ocean had been busy, but once the Muslim Arabs united the coasts from Egypt to India it flourished as never before. They set up trading posts as far south as Sufalah in Mozambique, east into the heart of the Indonesian archipelago, and north along the Chinese coast at least as far as Formosa. Persians, Indians, The cargoes carried in those rugged ships of sewn planks were both mundane and exotic. Among the goods that flowed into the Muslim Caliph's court at Baghdad were precious woods, ivory, amber, jewels and slaves from East Africa, porcelain and silk from China, ebony, pearls and gold from the Philippines, spices from the Moluccas, tin, silver, perfumes, camphor, drugs and sword blades from Malaysia and Indonesia.

On and beyond the fringes of this huge area were semi-mythical lands where sailing heroes like Sindbad set their extraordinary adventures. Even in the Indian Ocean itself there were enough hazards from freak storms, whales, cannibal islands and hidden reefs, to justify the most extravagant of mariner's tales.

There were other difficulties too. Arab trade with China declined after the foreign merchants in Canton were wiped out during a Chinese civil war, while earthquakes, religious conflicts and a bloody rising by the oppressed slaves of southern Iraq disrupted business in the Persian Gulf.

Yet in the 15th century the Arabs Chinese and Sumatrans also took part, the latter even colonizing Madagascar across almost 4000 miles of open ocean.

were still the leading merchants and sailors of this ocean. Then, in AD 1498, a famous seafarer named Shihab al Din Ahmad ibn Majid, author of one of the best Arabic nautical directories, met some strange European ships at Malindi in East Africa.

Their crews were Portuguese, their captain was none other than Vasco da Gama, and they had sailed right around Africa. Shihab al Din agreed to pilot these Portuguese across the Indian Ocean to India. It was the beginning of the end of Arab maritime glory.

Once Vasco da Gama's reports of the wealth of India reached home, other European sailors and pirates followed in his wake. The Arabs, Indians and Chinese fought back, yet they could not compete with the bigger and better armed European ships.

The dhows still survive, plying the coasts of Arabia and East Africa. They are, however, a very pale reflection of the glorious days of Sindbad the Sailor, Muhammad ibn Babishad and Shihab al Din Ahmad.

A famous Arab seafarer agreed to pilot the Portuguese explorer Vasco da Gama across the Indian Ocean – and begin a massive invasion by Europeans seeking the fabulous riches of India.

A CRAFT FOR IDLE HANDS

Up to the early nineteenth century, ivory and horn were used extensively for containers as well as numerous other useful items. Some of these implements were engraved and the craft eventually became universally known as Scrimshaw. Ivory and horn were expensive commodities so the development of metal and, later, synthetic materials, replaced them. As a result the art of Scrimshaw faded and all but died, that is, until recent years, when a revival started creating an interest in the craft once again.

Examples of the art can be found on sixteenth and seventeenth century firearms, many of which contained ornate inlays of bone or ivory engraved to the personal specifications of the owner. The practice found its way to America, where it became widespread during the French and Indian Wars of 1756 to 1763. Animal horn was the driest, most convenient way of carrying gunpowder for muskets. Professional hunters soon found a ready market for horn as explorers and settlers moved west and they sold their wares through gunsmiths or general stores.

Before selling the horns the hunters would make them hollow by removing the unwanted core, first by boiling then scraping it out. After this the inside area was shaped with sand or a rasp until it was paper thin or nearly transparent. The large end was plugged with hardwood, metal or animal skin, making it light and waterproof.

Before long it became a tradition for the backwoodsmen to engrave their powder horns. This was done either with the point of a sharp hunting knife or a red hot needle.

The owner's name, coupled with a verse or phrase relating to his travels along with the floral designs, could be found on many. But most preferred to engrave maps of the uncharted terrain and rivers they explored. Forts, then settlements, were added as civilisation moved further west.

Adept artists were much in demand and many were paid handsomely for their skills. The professional worker would polish the horn by rubbing oil into the surface with the palm of his hand. He might then pencil the design onto the surface before commencing to cut with an awl or graver, a type of small sharp chisel.

The engraver held the horn steady

Powder horns were often engraved with the owner's name, in this case Thadeus Bennitt who served from 1757 to 1758 in a fort in the heart of Indian country. The horn also showed the number of the fort, No. 4, and bore an incorrectly spelt phrase, "The Rose is Red The Vilet Blue and a Fols (fool's) Love Cannot Be Tru".

Other engravers preferred decorative designs like that shown on this Scottish cannon-size horn of 1683.

One of the finest engraving arts was started by explorers and seamen

by placing it in his lap and securing it with a strap looped over it then fixed to his foot. As he worked he would rub the cut marks with his soiled fingers to check the progress then, on completion, the design would be filled in with grease or vegetable oil mixed with soot or gunpowder dust and left to harden.

In Demand

Colour would be introduced by extracting dye-stuffs from plants, leaves, berries and fruit. A good engraver was much in demand in the military forts or camps, where he could exchange his work to avoid guard duties or fatigues, as well as for extra food and drink.

It is not known exactly how the term "Scrimshaw" came to be applied to the craft, but the word

"Scrimshirk" comes from the ancient Celtic language meaning "Idle Worker" and we now associate "shirk" with avoiding any task. Carving on ivory can be traced more readily to the seamen on the old whaling ships that sailed on long voyages spending years at sea. To pass long hours of boredom some would carve or whittle away designs on the ships planking. Many ships in the early 1800s were small and cramped containing between 40 and 90 men who often rioted or mutinied against their captains during the hours of inactivity. It was noticed that many crew members were engraving on whale's teeth as a pastime using knives or sail needles for tools.

The activity became a popular, soothing hobby, so before long the captains of cargo and military ships ensured that they left port with an

ample supply of whale's teeth to keep their crews occupied.

Fighting ships also used powder horns, large ones for priming their cannons, and these were often decorated with drawings of ships in full sail, sea-birds or fish. Inks, also ships paints in various colours, were used to embellish the designs. At one time it was thought that the Eskimos introduced Scrimshaw to the Western world, but it is highly likely that the craft was brought to them by those who sailed the high seas.

The art has now become popular again, especially in America, where firearms owners are personalising their collections with elaborate ivory inlays decorated with Scrimshaw. Some of the leading art colleges are now teaching the subject. There is now a great demand for the original gravers and ornate ink bottles of the early 19th century period.

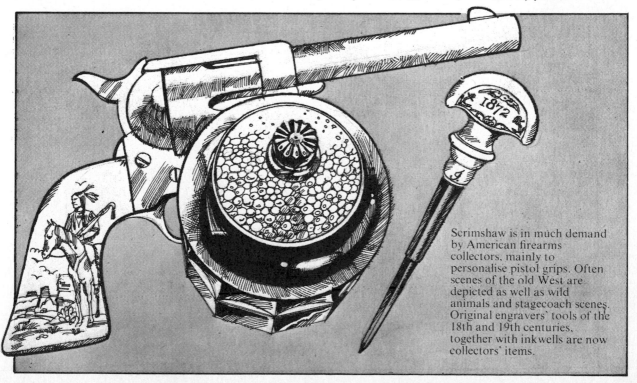

Scrimshaw is in much demand by American firearms collectors, mainly to personalise pistol grips. Often scenes of the old West are depicted as well as wild animals and stagecoach scenes. Original engravers' tools of the 18th and 19th centuries, together with inkwells are now collectors' items.

MYSTERY VOYAGE

She was the latest ship of the Blue Anchor Line to be launched, and her owners were proud of her, rightly so, for she was an impressive big twin-screw ship with three decks fore and aft. Moreover, she had been fitted with all the latest equipment. Her name was the *Waratah*.

One man, however, did not share in the owners' enthusiasm for the ship. This man, perhaps, rather surprisingly was Captain Ibery, her commander, a highly experienced sailor who had been employed by the company for over 40 years. After his maiden voyage in her, Captain Ibery had told his friends that he was well satisfied with the ship's performance. What he did *not* tell them was that he had complained to the owners of the inability of the *Waratah* to move in dock without ballast.

No one seems to have taken a great deal of notice of the Captain's complaint, for the *Waratah* set sail on her second voyage in April, 1909, after only a few minor repairs had been carried out. The ship's company in all numbered 119.

After calling in at the Australian ports, the *Waratah* reached Durban, where she took on 92 passengers and some more cargo which gave her a total load of 10,000 tons. Her next port of call was Cape Town. On her way there she passed another ship, the *Clan MacIntyre*. There was an exchange of friendly greetings by signal between the two ships, and then the *Waratah* sailed on her way – never to be seen again.

There was no undue concern at Cape Town when the *Waratah* did not arrive on the day she was due. After all, there were many reasons why she might have been late. She could have been held up at Durban, or developed some minor engine trouble in mid-ocean, for instance. It was not as if she were some leaky old tub. She was the latest and best cargo ship the Blue Anchor line had built. She would, no doubt, put into port the next day, or at the very latest, the day after.

The days passed and other ships came in which had started out from Durban after the *Waratah*. When they reported that they had seen no sign of her although they had been

travelling in the same shipping lane, everyone was forced to face the inescapable fact that the *Waratah* had disappeared.

Presumably she had sunk. But how? On the day after she had met the *Clan MacIntyre*, a storm had sprung up which one captain described as the most severe storm within living memory in those waters. Was it possible that the *Waratah* had failed to sail through it when all the other ships in its path had survived.

No Sign

In an attempt to find the answer, the seas were scoured for several weeks. But nothing was found – not a single spar, lifeboat or dead body. It was as if the sea had opened its waters and completely swallowed up the *Waratah*.

Eventually, a Board of Enquiry was held in London. At the end of two months of listening to the evidence, the Court could give no better explanation as to where, when and why the *Waratah* sank, than to say in effect that she had

been sunk "by an act of God".

After all this time is it possible for us to find out what happened to this vessel?

If one sifts through all the theories that were put forward, only one seems to make sense. The *Waratah* was an unstable, top heavy vessel with a bad list which made her turn turtle during the great storm.

This view was put forward at the time, but the experts at the Enquiry declared that the loss of the *Waratah* could not in any way have been blamed on her construction. She had been passed on five separate inspections and on each occasion no defect of any sort had been reported.

For all that, the fact remains that the *Waratah* did sink. One has to bear in mind, too, that if she was as stable as everyone had claimed she was, her 'death' by any other cause would have surely been a slow one, which would have left some traces on the water. Only by turning turtle and plunging to the bottom of the ocean in a matter of seconds, could she have carried everything and

everybody to the bottom without leaving a trace.

The 'turning turtle' theory is to some degree supported by her captain's comments to the owners after her first voyage. Much more important than that, however, is the evidence that was put forward by a man who actually sailed on the *Waratah* on her final voyage.

The gentleman concerned was a Mr Claude Sawyer, who joined the ship at Sydney, with the intention of sailing on her to Cape Town. He left the ship instead at Durban, from where he sent a telegram to his wife in which he said: *Thought Waratah top heavy. Landed Durban.*

Later, Mr Sawyer was much more explicit. The ship, he declared had rolled so excessively and so much that when she righted herself she did so with such violence that a number of the passengers had been flung off their feet. On one occasion when he was in his bath, he noted from the level of his water that the ship was lying on her side at an angle of about 45 degrees.

Disturbing as all this was to Mr Sawyer, what made him finally

leave the ship was a nightmare in which he saw an apparition in period dress holding a long sword in his right hand and a blood-stained rag in the other. After seeing this apparition in his dreams on three occasions Mr Sawyer came to the conclusion that this was some kind of warning, and he decided then to leave the ship at the first possible opportunity.

A nightmare which sent a man fleeing from a ship has no bearing on the mystery of how the *Waratah* sank. But his comments on the behaviour of the ship do, especially when they were supported by the comments of some of those who had travelled on the ship on her maiden voyage. They said that the ship had listed and rolled heavily. To be fair there were also others who claimed that her rolling had not been excessive.

All that is certain is that the *Waratah* sank at sea off the coast of South Africa, and the disaster was so swift and terrible that there was no opportunity for any of the boats to be launched. And there we have to let the matter rest.

Chewing gum became even more popular when an enterprising American salesman got King Edward VII to accept the gift of a packet. The story soon got around that it had received the Royal seal of approval and then everybody wanted to chew gum.

SOMETHING TO CHEW

Whether you chew gum just for fun, to help clean your teeth, or even to relax – different people give different reasons – chewing gum has become increasingly popular all over the world.

On average every American citizen chews 300 sticks *each* year. In Japan the figure is not too far behind, around 250, and in Britain the figure is close to 200 sticks.

In Russia tourists use it as 'tips' – much preferred to cash by some Russians who are prepared to pay almost £2 for a five-stick pack of gum which cost about 8p in Britain. A newspaper correspondent giving this information also said he was stopped in his car on some pretext by a policeman who, like lots of others over there, seems to think that tourists'·pockets are lined with chewing gum.

Ask your father when people first started to chew gum and he'll probably tell you it was during the Second World War, when American soldiers made it popular in Britain.

In fact, people have been chewing gum for over a thousand years.

An ancient Indian people in Central America, the Mayas, were the first known chewers of gum. They created a remarkable civilisation about the second century AD, which lasted until the Spanish conquest of that part of the world.

And they discovered that chewing gum helped to quench their thirst, and to keep their teeth beautifully white.

They made their gum by boiling the sap of the Sapodilla tree, which grows in the tropical rain forests of Central America. The sap is known as chicle. This was the word for juice in the language of the Aztecs, who were neighbours of the Mayas.

Today, chicle is still the most common base for chewing gum.

People who have made scientific studies of the subject have found more reasons for the popularity of chewing gum, apart from the thirst-quenching, teeth-cleaning ones enjoyed by the Mayas.

It seems that the act of chewing eases tense nerves and muscles. When people are nervous, or bored, chewing brings relief.

A study by Professor H. L. Hollingsworth, of Columbia University in the United States, in the 1940s, showed that chewing relaxes people while they are working. And modern chewing gum provides this benefit in a convenient, hygienic and flavoursome form.

It also helps to keep people alert. In fact, chewing gum was supplied by Britain to its armed forces in both World Wars for this reason. As early as 1914, the British Government bought one million packets of gum for its troops.

The manufacturers go to a lot of trouble to ensure that their gum has all these qualities.

First, the chicle is collected from the Sapodilla tree by 'chicleros', who cut grooves in the bark in a herringbone pattern, so that the chicle flows smoothly down into canvas bags tied to the foot of the tree. Other gum bases are used for modern chewing gum, but chicle is still the most important.

Then the chicle is boiled in large stainless steel pots over wood fires, and poured into moulds, so that it hardens into solid blocks which are easy to transport.

These blocks are carried by mules or canoe from the chicleros' camp to the sea ports of Central America, from where they are shipped to manufacturers all over the world.

When the blocks of chicle reach the factory, they are ground, and melted in large, steam-jacketed kettles.

Then, the sterilised gum base is thoroughly purified by pumping it through fine mesh screens, centrifuge machines, and ultra-fine pressure strainers. At this stage, it looks like a thick syrup.

Next, it goes to the mixers, which are huge vessels with rotating blades, holding about 1,500 pounds of gum base. It is mixed here with powdered sugar, syrup and flavour, at just the right time, and in just the right amounts. Each different brand of gum has a different recipe, which must be carefully followed to give perfect results.

HOW CHEWING GUM IS MADE

INFORMATION SUPPLIED BY
THE WRIGLEY COMPANY LTD

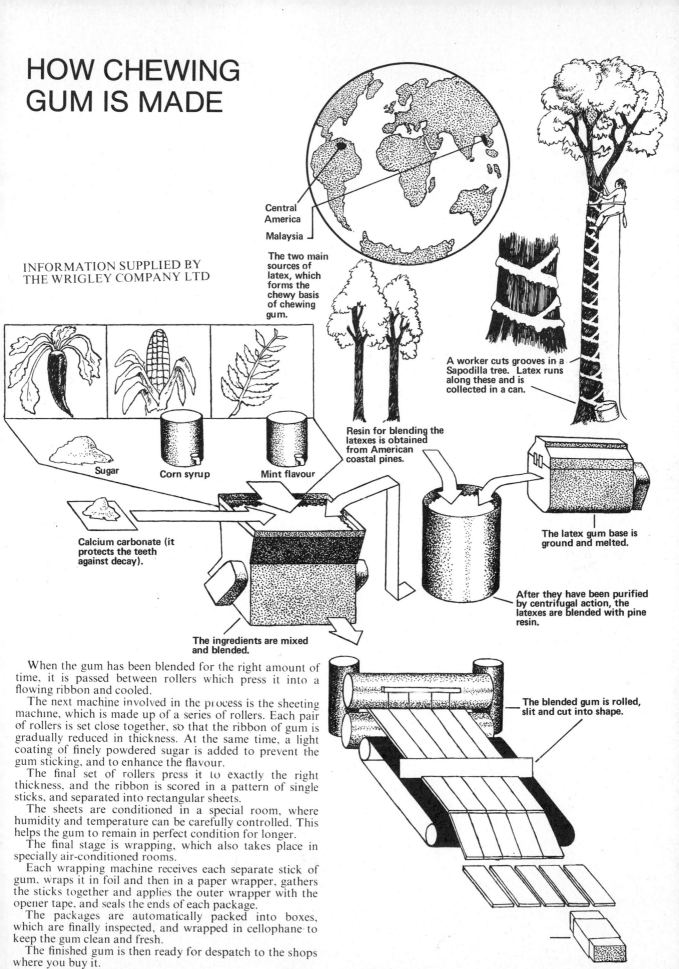

Central America

Malaysia

The two main sources of latex, which forms the chewy basis of chewing gum.

A worker cuts grooves in a Sapodilla tree. Latex runs along these and is collected in a can.

Resin for blending the latexes is obtained from American coastal pines.

Sugar

Corn syrup

Mint flavour

Calcium carbonate (it protects the teeth against decay).

The latex gum base is ground and melted.

After they have been purified by centrifugal action, the latexes are blended with pine resin.

The ingredients are mixed and blended.

The blended gum is rolled, slit and cut into shape.

When the gum has been blended for the right amount of time, it is passed between rollers which press it into a flowing ribbon and cooled.

The next machine involved in the process is the sheeting machine, which is made up of a series of rollers. Each pair of rollers is set close together, so that the ribbon of gum is gradually reduced in thickness. At the same time, a light coating of finely powdered sugar is added to prevent the gum sticking, and to enhance the flavour.

The final set of rollers press it to exactly the right thickness, and the ribbon is scored in a pattern of single sticks, and separated into rectangular sheets.

The sheets are conditioned in a special room, where humidity and temperature can be carefully controlled. This helps the gum to remain in perfect condition for longer.

The final stage is wrapping, which also takes place in specially air-conditioned rooms.

Each wrapping machine receives each separate stick of gum, wraps it in foil and then in a paper wrapper, gathers the sticks together and applies the outer wrapper with the opener tape, and seals the ends of each package.

The packages are automatically packed into boxes, which are finally inspected, and wrapped in cellophane to keep the gum clean and fresh.

The finished gum is then ready for despatch to the shops where you buy it.

One of the rumours concerning Bierce's disappearance suggests that he met up with Pancho Villa and offered his services, but was rejected and shot by order of the Mexican revolutionary leader.

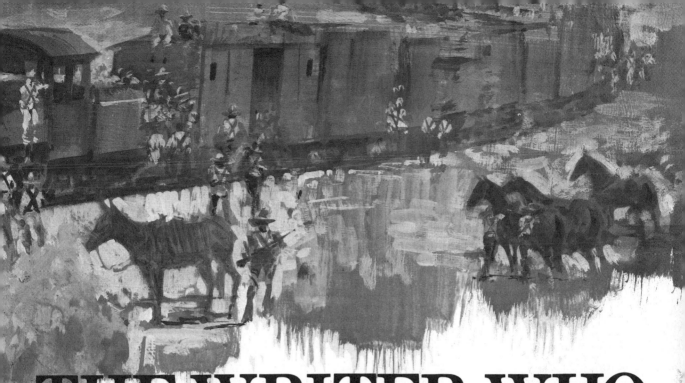

THE WRITER WHO
LIKED FIGHTING

"IF you should hear of my being stood up against a Mexican stone wall and shot to rags, please know that I think it is a pretty good way to go. It beats old age, disease or falling down the cellar stairs."

These were some of the last words that Ambrose Bierce – "Bitter Bierce" was one of his politer nicknames – wrote before mysteriously vanishing into a Mexico wracked by revolution. The great storyteller and possessor of the most poisonous pen in American history also wrote in those last days: "I like fighting: I want to see it." He was 71!

Ambrose Bierce was a literary giant and a literary monster. Though the most famous thing he ever did was to vanish, he had earlier made himself the most hated and feared journalist in America.

This handsome, strange man, who viciously attacked politicians, the Church, presidents, generals, in fact nearly all authority, as well as harmless enough poets and writers and many men and most women, was born in Ohio in 1842. He was the tenth of 13 children, disliking most of them, and his parents, especially his father. Birth to him was "the first and direst of all disasters". Not that he had a high opinion of himself. In *The Devil's Dictionary*, which he compiled, he included such acid word definitions as *ALONE – in bad company* and *BRUTE – see husband.* He called a novel *'a short story padded out'*, a *SAINT – a dead sinner revised and edited* and *a QUILL – an implement of torture yielded by a goose and wielded by an ass!* For Bierce, it seems, success was the one unpardonable sin.

Yet, his appalling family and married life apart, he was a success. After an odd childhood in which his lack of education was balanced by a spell on a local newspaper in Indiana, he found true happiness as a soldier, and a very brave one, in the Civil War (1861-5), fighting for the North. He despised ambitious generals who were prepared to sacrifice men for personal and political ambitions, but he did not despise his fellow soldiers, or

even the enemy, and twice saved wounded men under fire.

One of these rescues took place in 1826 when Bierce was a lieutenant in the Ninth Indiana army. Its commander, Major J. D. Braden, was shot in the head during a furious attack by the Confederates.

Bierce, usually cold and unapproachable, knelt beside the major and gripped his hand and cried with a sudden unleashing of pent up emotion.

Then, despite the bullets that were flying around them, Bierce picked up the major and carried him to safety.

Later, the finest and most realistic stories Bierce wrote were about war. They were some of the best war short stories ever written.

After the war he had a spell as a government employee in the defeated South which put him off governments for ever and made him sympathise with the vanquished. This did not stop him having to defend a steamboat almost single-handed from a Southern gang who tried to board her and seize the cotton aboard to prevent it going to the hated Northerners. The only help he got was from a Southerner whom he had allowed on for a free ride.

"Why did you help me fight your own people?" he asked the tough ex-soldier.

"Well, Cap," said the man, "You took me aboard for nothing, so I thought I'd work my passage!"

Next followed a spell of surveying in the wildest West, then he settled in San Francisco to become a living legend, or nightmare, some would have said.

Let it be stressed that Bierce was not always an ogre *privately*, for he had a number of friends and cronies and he did help young writers of talent. Older ones, unless, like Mark Twain, they were in the genius class, were normally savaged in print. Not surprisingly, he carried a six-shooter at all times!

His worst exploit was a verse he published in one of William Randolph Hearst's muck-raking papers in 1900. A Kentucky governor-elect named Goebel had been shot dead and Bierce, who hated the president, William

McKinley (more or less on principle), produced this:
The bullet that pierced Goebel's breast
Cannot be found in all the West;
Good reason, it is speeding here
To stretch McKinley on his bier.

A few months later McKinley was assassinated by a mad anarchist, but Bierce's enemies and even some friends blamed him for inspiring the killing. One good result was that it helped ruin Hearst's chances of becoming president himself. This was an excellent thing, for though Hearst was a brilliant, if unsavoury, newspaperman, he was power-mad and was partly responsible for making the United States fight Spain over Cuba in 1898.

As for Bierce, he got more and more bored with life. One of his sons was killed in a gunfight over a girl, the other had died, and so had his wife, all of whom he had shamefully neglected. His bad asthma made him more depressed, so, in December 1913, having put his affairs in order, he crossed into Mexico "to see the fighting" in the revolution.

At that moment, the revolution that was raging had developed into a ferocious power struggle between rivals. General Huerta, having murdered President Madero, was faced with powerful regional chiefs, the most dangerous of whom was Pancho Villa, and it was towards Villa that Bierce seemed to be heading, carrying credentials as an observer, and, more dangerously, 1,500 dollars, a suicidal amount in a bandit-ridden land, totally without law.

His last letter, to a friend in Washington, said: "Trainload of troops leaving Chihuahua every day. Expect next day to go to Ojinaga, partly by rail." And that is the last thing known about him.

Did he leave Chihuahua City as planned? Probably. But there was a gap in the line 60 miles from the city, which is near Texas, and he may have set out on foot to join Villa's army, besieging Ojinaga. One of Villa's men later recognised a photograph of Bierce, so perhaps he died as he wished to the sound of the guns which he loved as others love symphonic music. He may lie in a mass grave, or under a mound somewhere, his money stolen after death.

Ludicrous stories kept circulating about him, however, the unlikeliest being that he had gone to England to advise Lord Kitchener about the conduct of the First World War! A less stupid one was that he had quarrelled with Villa and been shot after offering his services. As he did not like revolutionaries, and as there were plenty of Americans around Villa to know if the famous Bierce was

Bierce, together with a fellow passenger, once defended a river boat carrying cotton against attack by a Southern gang who were determined to stop the cargo reaching its destination in the north.

there too, that rumour is also almost certainly a false one. None of Villa's relations have recalled that Bierce knew Villa. Optimists think he looked at the war, did not like it, and headed for the Andes where the air could be good for his asthma, but there is no foundation for such an idea. More probably he died on the way to the siege of Ojinaga, if he was not killed during it. Perhaps he was attacked by bandits and possibly lay wounded with other victims of the war, or he expired alone, trying to reach water. The best thing that can have happened to him would have been a quick death from a bullet. Which is just the sort of death this extraordinary man may have planned for himself.

Amid a hail of bullets, Bierce carried a wounded comrade to safety.

JAWS OF DEATH

In Los Angeles in California there is a small park, and in this park there is a small lake surrounded by railings. The lake looks quite like any other but is, in fact, a pool of tar. There are other such lakes in this locality, which is known as Ranco-La-Brea.

These pools lay in the middle of a vast desolate plain 140,000 years ago. Dust naturally collected on the tarry surface and when rain fell the tar lakes became natural but treacherous reservoirs. From miles around the animals smelled the water and hurried to slake their thirst. The sticky tar trapped these poor creatures. Their cries of distress soon attracted the attention of the flesh-eating animals, who in turn became bogged down in the tar, whilst attempting to make an easy kill.

Through the course of time the tar has protected the bones of these unfortunate creatures, preserving them so well that scientists can even find on them evidence of the diseases they suffered from.

One of the animal remains found in this way was that of the sabre-toothed carnivore known as Smilodon. Practically all the Smilodon skeletons found in the tar pools were those of young and inexperienced Smilodons, the more experienced being too intelligent to hunt their prey in this way.

The most striking feature of the Smilodon was its pair of sabre-shaped canines, which were sharpened along the rear edge and grew to a length of about 150mm. When the mouth was closed, these fearsome weapons projected far down on either side of the lower jaw. To make full use of them the beast had to open his mouth very wide and to do this he was aided by the special way in which his lower jaw was attached to his skull.

No-one could doubt that Smilodon caused much alarm and fear wherever he travelled, hunting the early forms of horse, gazelles, antelopes and even the enormous Mastodon. His large scale destruction of herbivorous animals might well have aided in their extinction. Their extinction in turn might well have brought about his own disappearance.

HE SET THE WORLD WORKING

"Get off that floor at once, Jamie, or you'll be coughing again all night. It's damp and cold. I'm sure you can do your drawings on your slate just as well."

Mrs Watt, mother of the delicate Jamie, was naturally angry. Her son was too unwell to go to school in the winter, and it was a constant problem to keep him occupied.

Paper for drawing was expensive—particularly in those hard times for Scotland, with English soldiers invading the country, and the Scottish victory of Preston Pans so soon followed by the terrible defeat at Culloden.

But the lines and circles young James drew on the heavy flagstones of the kitchen floor were not just childish drawings, as his father and mother believed.

For, in one of the brief periods when he was well enough to go to school, Jamie had got a glimpse of the science of geometry.

From that painstaking work in chalk on his mother's kitchen floor James Watt set out on the road to make his name immortal among engineers.

The legend is that this thoughtful boy obtained the idea for a steam engine when the steam lifted the lid of his mother's kettle. But in later life he never mentioned such an incident.

Geometry, and all the careful measuring that it involved, remained his passion.

In 1755, partly to escape from the damp climate, and also because he wanted to be in touch with the finest scientific brains in the country, he set off for London when he was in his teens.

In London he got a job with a scientific-instrument maker, helping to produce and assemble sextants, compasses and other ships' devices, as well as ordinary geometrical instruments.

He did so well that in a few years he was able to return to Scotland, where he set up his own instrument-making shop in Glasgow.

The professors of Glasgow University were delighted to have such a useful craftsman available, and he was appointed official instrument-maker to the university.

One day the university asked him to repair a model of a Newcomen pumping engine used to instruct the technical students. Some of them, playing with the model, had broken it.

The Newcomen engine was a cumbersome but useful device which had been used to pump water out of mines.

It was not a steam engine in a real sense. It had no wheels and instead of using the *power* of steam it used only its heat.

A heavy counterweight pulled the

James Watt.

piston to the top of the cylinder. A small boy then turned a tap and let steam into the cylinder below the piston.

He then turned off the steam and turned another tap to play cold water over the cylinder. This condensed the steam and created a vacuum, which pulled the piston down.

James was a Scotsman, and he hated waste. The Newcomen idea of making the cylinder hot one moment and dousing it with cold water the next seemed to him a terribly spendthrift way of using the energy of burning wood or coal.

For two years he worked on alternative ideas.

One idea led to another until he not only cut out the waste of the original Newcomen engine, but by admitting the steam into the top and bottom of the cylinder, and controlling it with valves he made a true steam engine, using the power to drive the piston up and down.

Into the picture next came Dr John Roebuck, who was worried by the fact that water was flooding into several of the coal mines he owned.

He had heard of young James Watt and went to see him in his workshop. He was so impressed by the young Scottish inventor that he decided to finance him. Watt went to work in the out-buildings of Roebuck's mansion.

This was a dark era in Watt's life. He was often ill, dissatisfied with his work and made no real progress. Roebuck's fortune went down and down, until finally the mine owner failed altogether. His financial interest in Watt's inventions went to a metal goods manufacturer, Matthew Boulton, of Soho, Birmingham.

For Watt, this was the turning point. Boulton was the man who gave Watt his big chance, who saw looming in the young Scotsman's mind the final steps which would harness steam and make it drive machinery.

It meant that for the first time since the dawn of history, things could be made to move without using sheer physical strength, apart from the limited application of the water-wheel or windmill.

Thanks to Watt's inventive genius, industrial Britain and the world were given the power to turn the machines in factories and mills.

Boulton had a magnificent engineering works. He could make anything that Watt designed.

The first engines were just improved pumps, but in 1781 Watt patented a device to turn the up-and-down movement of the piston into the rotary movement of a wheel. This was the steam engine, the unit of *power*.

Talkative workmen in the factory spread the news, and others rushed inventions through.

Just to show his contempt for these dishonest imitators, Watt retired to his office and invented *five* different ways of getting rotary motion from his engine.

Wealth and fame were his. His engines went into the new factories of the textile industry and enabled hundreds of mines to be pumped dry.

Before he died in 1819 boats powered by steam engines were sailing the seas and steam locomotives were hauling wagons at collieries.

Strange Man

James Watt remained a strange and not very happy man until his death at the age of eighty-three. "My only pleasures have been idleness and sleep," he told friends.

But he was never idle and his constant ill-health rarely allowed him a good night's rest. His inventive mind was perpetually seeking out new ideas.

Few people now realize, for instance, that this remarkable Scotsman was the inventor of copying ink, that he took some crude photographs through the action of silver nitrate exposed to light, and first worked out the formula for horse-power – which he did, characteristically, by getting carthorses to pull at different weights.

All sorts of memorials exist to this famous man. Without doubt, the one which he would have liked best is that his name, or at least the initial W, appears on every electric light bulb.

A watt is a unit of electricity, and so named in honour of the man who not only harnessed the earlier power of steam, but laid down the formula for calculating the work done by any machine in terms of horse-power.

The electrical unit would have mystified Watt himself – but how he would have enjoyed puzzling it out!

THE TINY TUNNELLER

Voles can be easily distinguished from mice by their short blunt faces and smaller eyes and ears. The bank-vole is the smallest and most attractive of the British species. Once known as the red-backed meadow-mouse, it has a bright reddish coloured back and pale underparts, varying locally from pure white to grey tinged with yellow. It's tail is a pale brown, covered with fine hairs.

Preferring rather dry ground, the favoured habitats of the bank-vole are deciduous woods or copses with plenty of ground cover and in many parts of the country hedgerow banks, covered with ivy or other low vegetation, will be honeycombed with their tunnels. They are also common in most country gardens.

Active by day and night, bank-voles are agile creatures often climbing small trees and bushes in search of nuts, berries, young leaves and buds; they are however less vegetarian than other voles. Insects and snails account for about a third of their diet.

Bank-voles excavate extensive networks of winding tunnels, close to the surface of the ground. Sometimes these tunnels are only covered by fallen leaves. They have many exits and short branches and these are often used for storing large quantities of berries and nuts.

Small ball-shaped nests are constructed from finely shredded grass and bark, and lined with moss or wool. They are usually hidden in a depression under a bush or in the roots of a tree, but nests above ground in old birds' nests, especially those of wrens, are not uncommon.

The main breeding season normally extends from about the middle of April to October. Four or five litters a year are usual, each consisting of from three to seven young. The gestation period is normally 18 to 19 days, but since females often become pregnant again immediately after giving birth, this may be prolonged by a few days to enable the previous litter to be weaned. The young are born naked and blind, their eyes open in 9-10 days and they are independant in about three weeks and can be sexually mature in as little as five to six weeks.

Although bank-voles seldom reach plague proportions they do have cycles of abundance and in a favourable year a single pair could have as many as two hundred decendants. But they would not all be likely to survive for bank voles are the prey of many predators. These include birds like the kestrel, owl and buzzard, and mammals like the fox, stoat and the weasel which can follow it along its tunnels.

The bank-vole is widely distributed throughout the British mainland although it tends to thin out in the north-east of England and in Scotland.

THE AUTOMATION REVOLUTION

There is virtually no part of our daily lives that is not affected by automation.

The word "automation" is defined in the dictionary as "automatic control of successive production processes by the use of electronic equipment", but the word is usually used in a more general sense.

The first part of the word comes from a Greek word *automatos*, which means "acting by itself", and so automation, or automatic control, means some mechanical, electrical or chemical device that carries out a routine task which would normally be done by a human being.

Throughout his development, Man has tried to make life's routine tasks easier by devising and building machines that would do the work for him. Some early examples of these would include perhaps watermills and windmills, which could operate simple machinery without any help from man.

Some later models of these mills had a governor built into them—a device that prevented the machinery they were driving from going too fast by applying a brake. This came into operation automatically.

One of the most successful automatic control devices was invented by a boy called Humphrey Potter, who was employed in a coal mine during the 18th century. His job was to open two valves in succession which allowed steam to enter and escape from a beam engine used for pumping water out of the mine.

The young boy soon became tired of his boring and repetitive job, so he attached lengths of cord from the valve handles to the ends of the beam which rocked to and fro as the engine worked, and when properly adjusted they opened the valves at just the right moment and did the work for him.

At the start of the 19th century, a Frenchman named Joseph Jacquard invented a system of needles and hooks which automatically selected the right coloured threads needed to make a pattern in a length of cloth passing through a loom.

Previously it was necessary for the weaver to watch the pattern as it was being formed and then shout out to another man which threads of the warp had to be lifted at the right moment, and so the Jacquard Loom was another step forward in automation.

Dial a number on your telephone and a highly automated system sends your call swiftly to its destination.

Of course, all these early examples of automation seem crude when compared with the highly sophisticated techniques which are today being applied in so many different fields of industry and modern technology. So advanced has automation become that it is now possible for whole factories to operate with only a few men pressing buttons or moving switches.

Complicated automation of this kind has only become possible since the invention and perfection of the computer—those amazing electronic "brains" which can be programmed to carry out an almost infinite number of complex tasks without the need of human beings other than a few to monitor their progress.

Computers, or calculators, might be said to have originated from the abacus—a simple framework of wood with beads threaded on lengths of wire on which the ancient Romans did all their arithmetic. An even earlier method of counting was to store pebbles in a leather or cloth bag, and in fact the Latin word for pebble is *calculus*, from which our modern word calculate is derived.

The first calculating machine was invented in the mid-17th century by a young French mathematician called Blaise Pascal. It consisted of a series of gear wheels rather similar to those used in a clock, and numbers were fed into it by rotating the spindles of the gears. It was a clever idea for speeding up calculations, but if Pascal were alive today he would be astonished at both the small size and the speed of operation of today's calculators with their integrated circuits and silicon chips.

Computers are being applied to an ever increasing number of industrial processes, and they are increasingly affecting our lives in ways which we frequently don't realise. Computers are able to store information fed into them—they have memories, and that information can be called upon whenever the operator requires it. Information fed into a computer can also be processed.

An example of what is called data processing is used in many American supermarkets. When the goods are being costed by the girl at the checkout, every time she punches a key, her keyboard sends electronic impulses to a large computer which may be many miles away.

The following morning, staff at the computer centre watch as it adds up all the totals of the different goods sold in the supermarkets the previous day, and by pressing another button or two, the operator can estimate the number of replacement items which will be needed to restock the supermarket shelves.

Computers have brought automation to a number of non-industrial areas such as police forces. Information already known about people who have committed crimes is stored in the computer's memory banks, and when a person is being questioned about a crime, the police can "ask" the computer to tell them if similar crimes have been committed, and if so, does the description of their suspect match with anyone arrested previously.

Computers are also widely used in today's jet-powered air liners. Placed in a handy position on the flight deck, all relevant navigational information needed about the flight can be programmed into them, what altitude to fly at, when to change course, when to reduce height, when to increase or reduce speed in order to arrive at the pre-arranged time. Computers can also be used to assist a landing in bad weather.

The world of medicine has also been automated to some extent. By fastening electrodes, for example, to the pulse and heart of a patient, or a number of patients, it is possible for a doctor or nurse to monitor their condition from a cubicle outside the ward. If a patient who has a serious heart condition suffers a sudden attack, the machine will respond by triggering off an alarm.

Computers are also being used as a help in diagnosing disease. A mass of information about known symptoms of a number of diseases is stored in the

There is no need for an attendant at many of today's car parks. Automatic barriers control both entrance and exit, and collect the parking fee as well!

In this illustration a nurse is monitoring temperatures and supervising wards from one central position.

computer's memory, and when the doctor feeds in the patient's symptoms, the computer compares them with its programmed information, and comes up with alternative possibilities for the doctor to consider.

Each time you make a telephone call you are using a highly automated system of communication. Impulses of electric current in the form of a code are sent out as you operate the dial or push-button controls of the instrument. At the telephone exchange these are sorted out by the equipment and your call is routed to its destination.

It is even possible today to dial numbers in countries thousands of miles away with as little fuss as dialing the number of a neighbour or friend a few miles distant. Thousands of these international telephone calls make a journey out into space to man-made satellites orbiting over a fixed spot on the earth's surface.

This miracle of communication would not be possible without the miniaturised circuits formed by the tiny silicon chips. Some of these electronic circuits are so small they can be passed through the eye of a needle—even when there is a piece of thread in it!

Automation brings with it one great problem which has yet to be solved. As computer-controlled machines gradually take over the jobs previously done by sometimes hundred of men and women, a great deal of thought will have to be given to what happens to the people affected.

Even the humblest of jobs, such as a car park attendant, are now being done by a machine, and computer technologists calculate that apart from fully automated factories, the computer will soon move into offices, and even the home.

Who knows, perhaps one day in the not too distant future, parents will not have to worry about household chores. There will be a fully programmed robot to do all the work. It sounds fine, but shall we not all get bored to death by doing nothing except pressing buttons all day!

ONE HUMP

The two-humped camel comes from Western Asia

A hump—or two—is very useful to a camel. For it is in the hump that the camel stores the fat upon which it draws when other food supplies run short. There are two kinds of camels— the Arabian or single-humped camel of Arabia, Syria and Africa, and the Bactrian camel with two humps, of Western Asia.

At the end of a long, weary journey over barren land with scanty food, the camel will have used up most of its fat, and the hump will have almost vanished.

But a long rest and plenty of good food at the journey's end will restore the hump to its former size.

No animal is so valuable in the hot, dry parts of the world as the camel. With little to eat or drink, it can travel long distances across the great deserts of Africa or Asia without suffering from lack of

OR TWO...

The single-humped camel is found in Arabia, Syria and Africa.

food or water. The camel carries in special water cells in its roomy stomach enough water to last it for several days.

To save itself from being suffocated by the blinding sand storms, the camel can close its large nostrils, and it can also shield its eyes by specially thick, heavy eyelids.

Its feet are shod with soft, broad cushions, while its knees and breast are protected by thick, horny pads to prevent the skin being injured when it kneels down. Another form of camel is the dromedary. This is a highly-bred Arabian riding camel used for swift travelling, instead of as a pack animal.

With good reason have these animals been called ships of the desert, for they are unique in being able to survive for long periods on the vast sandy "seas".

Rumours were buzzing around Ireland. People said that the young Earl of Warwick, who had a good claim to the English throne, had escaped from the Tower of London, where he was being kept prisoner and had landed in Ireland.

The Irish were very pleased, for they did not like the Welsh Henry Tudor, who had defeated King Richard III in battle and been crowned King Henry VII.

The nobles and gentry of Ireland liked this pleasant, well-mannered youth and they became convinced that this lad really was the Earl of Warwick. He was proclaimed in Dublin as King Edward VI and crowned in the cathedral there.

Before long, news of this reached King Henry VII in England. He was more angry than alarmed, for the real Earl of Warwick was still his prisoner, in the Tower. Henry sent

for the young earl and had him paraded through the streets of London. He announced that anyone who wanted to, might speak to him, to make sure that he was the real Earl of Warwick.

This did not prevent the supporters of the false earl landing in England to fight for the crown, but the English people did not join them. They did not like this rebel band of wild Irishmen and German soldiers, hired

THE PRETENDER KINGS

Instead of executing Lambert Simnel, King Henry put him to work in the royal kitchen, turning the spit on which the meat was roasted.

72

from abroad.

King Henry led his soldiers to fight the rebels. In those days travel was not very easy, for there were no wide, paved main roads, kept in good repair, as there are today. People who lived in one part of the country often knew very little about the rest of the country. This was true of the Earl of Oxford, King Henry's general, who lost his way completely when the army was between Nottingham and Newark. It took five guides from a nearby village to put the army on the right road again.

They caught up with the rebels at the village of Stoke and had little difficulty in defeating them. The lad who had pretended to be the Earl of Warwick was captured. It was discovered that he was really the son of a joiner, who lived in Oxford and his real name was Lambert Simnel.

King Henry was a clever man. Instead of chopping off Simnel's head, which was the usual punishment for a rebel, he gave him a job in the royal kitchen. He thought that if people saw him around, hard at work, they would remember the rebellion and how miserably it had failed and would be less tempted to start plotting themselves.

One day, King Henry gave a great banquet, to which he invited many of his nobles. Some of them had taken part in the rebellion and as they sat at dinner, a serving boy brought round the wine. The embarrassed nobles who had been in the rebellion recognised him at once. It was Lambert Simnel.

A few years later, another, much more serious imposter claimed King Henry's throne. This time, the young man was abroad in Burgundy, where Henry could not reach him. He was a handsome, charming young man called Perkin Warbeck and he claimed to be Richard, Duke of York, the younger of the two princes who had been put in the Tower by their Uncle Richard.

Perkin Warbeck's story was that he was in the Tower, with his elder brother Edward, when their uncle was crowned king, as Richard III. Soon after he had been crowned, their uncle sent men to kill them, for they were the rightful heirs to the throne. Perkin Warbeck said that his brother, Edward, had actually been smothered, but the man who was sent to kill them was so horrified at his terrible task, that he had killed only Edward. He saved Richard and helped him to escape abroad.

This tale was a very good one and many people believed it, especially as Perkin Warbeck was given a home and money by the Duchess of Burgundy, who was the aunt of the young princes. The King of France and the King of Scotland also supported him and gave him money, for they were always ready to pick a

Perkin Warbeck was put in the stocks in London, where passers-by could go and look at him. There, he was made to read a confession, that he was not really Richard, Duke of York, as he had pretended.

quarrel with England and a few English noblemen went to join him.

Nobody really knew what had happened to the two little princes in the Tower. Two men confessed to having murdered them in the Tower and King Henry ordered men to see if they could find the bodies, but they had no success. The princes, it was said, had been buried secretly.

Henry could do nothing to prove that Perkin Warbeck was an impostor. Instead, he had to work hard to make treaties and trading agreements with Scotland, France and Burgundy, one of the conditions being that these countries did not give Perkin Warbeck a home.

Warbeck was driven from country to country. At last he landed in England and the Cornish people supported him. They were an

untrained, ill-armed mob and King Henry easily defeated them. Perkin Warbeck gave himself up and was kept a prisoner, but he was well treated and given a certain amount of freedom.

After a time, he escaped but he was quickly recaptured. King Henry had him put in the stocks in London for two days. While there, he had to read out a confession, that he was really an impostor, to the people who came to see him. Then he was put in the Tower.

Still there were plots and rumours and attempts to free Perkin Warbeck and the Earl of Warwick. King Henry was sure that while they were alive his throne was not really secure. Two years later, both of them were accused of treason, found guilty and executed.

THEY BEAT THE ATLANTIC

Arthur Whitten Brown

John Alcock

Some men are born with a natural instinct for their vocation. Some are born to be great footballers, great motor racing drivers, great artists.

Some men, too, are born to be great airmen. For them the splendid loneliness of the sky and the hazards and perils associated with reaching it are in the blood. They become so that they cannot live without it.

Such a man was John Alcock. At twenty he was a pilot and had already proved himself a born airman. In the first World War he flew in the Royal Navy Air Service and after flying in many raids won the Distinguished Service Cross.

Back in peace-time England Alcock had to continue flying – for flying was his life. And the big target for peace-time aviators was a non-stop flight across the Atlantic Ocean.

When a group of British airmen and mechanics decided to go to Newfoundland and prepare an aircraft for such a flight, Alcock and his friend Lieutenant Arthur Whitten Brown – like Alcock an R.A.F. officer went with them. Alcock had already made up his mind to attempt the first transatlantic flight with Brown as his navigator and a Vickers Vimy biplane as their aircraft.

At St. John's, Newfoundland, Alcock and Brown busied themselves about their twin-engined plane. They had fitted extra fuel tanks, capable of carrying 865 gallons of petrol and fifty gallons of oil, giving an estimated range of 2,440 miles. By the standards of that year, 1919, the Vimy, which had been designed as a wartime bomber, was a big plane, with a wingspan of some 21 metres and standing 4.5 metres high.

Five o'clock Saturday afternoon was fixed for the take-off. The two airmen ate a hurried meal standing by their plane; then they climbed aboard, started the two Rolls-Royce engines and bumped down the narrow field and into the air.

Gusts and currents buffeted the Vimy until she was able to fly high over open country. Then, as she reached the Atlantic, a strong, south-westerly wind blew on her tail and gave her extra push. The good effect of this was counteracted almost at once by the early airmen's most feared enemy – fog.

For Brown, sitting alongside his pilot so that he could speak with reasonable comfort above the steady thrumming of the engines and the whine of the wind in the wire rigging, good visibility was vital to make observations in checking and setting their course. But the fog closed in remorselessly, masking the sea, the sky and the horizon. The Vimy was flying blind – and in 1919 flying blind without any of the devices and instruments that were to come later, was a perilous adventure.

With straining eyes and taut

The statue at London's Heathrow Airport which commemorates Alcock and Brown's historic flight.

nerves Alcock fought to keep the stringbag Vimy on an even keel. Suddenly, at midnight, the sky cleared, showing the stars twinkling in the darkness around them. Brown pored over his navigational aids while Alcock levelled the plane with the horizon ahead of them. Then, as suddenly as the fog had gone, it was back again. And to add to their troubles the air-speed indicator failed.

With no means of ascertaining that anything might be wrong with the plane's flight, Alcock flew on into the impenetrable blanket. Only when the engine note rose and the plane trembled did he realize that the Vimy had gone into a dive and was spinning out of control towards the sea!

By an incredible stroke of luck the plane spiralled into a stretch of clear atmosphere. Glancing down Alcock saw that he had just sufficient height to pull the Vimy out of her spin. With the supreme skill of the born airman he brought the plane horizontal to the sea just above the waves.

Now to the perils of fog was added the nightmare of freezing air and blinding sleet. Soon treacherous ice was forming on the hinges of the ailerons, jamming them and depriving Alcock of all lateral control. The ice spread to cover the aircraft completely and even threatened to interfere with the engines by forming on the radiator shutters.

The vital air-speed indicator, which had been got working again, was now seized with ice. It was imperative in that thick fog that it should be working, and several times, at great risk to himself, Brown clambered out on to the wing

Brown had to climb out on the wing and chip away ice which was forming on the engine.

to chip ice from the instrument. But the ice had damaged the indicator, and it was no longer reliable.

At last came the dawn. So that Brown could make his vital observations, Alcock put the biplane into a dive through thick vapour towards the sea. Down, down, down went the Vimy, until suddenly it broke into clear air again, almost within touching distance of the sea. Alcock levelled out above the lonely ocean, where shafts of sun sparkling on the water drove the feeling of dead fatigue from the two men and imbued them with a sense of impending triumph.

Through the mist and light rain ahead of them Alcock saw two islands – Turbot and Eastal islands off the coast of Galway in Ireland. Soon they were passing over the islands and the sprawling countryside of Ireland below them.

For a while Alcock circled over the green fields, signalling with Very lights. When he found a likely meadow in which to land he turned the Vimy's head to wind, idled her engines and dipped her nose. Gently the biplane skimmed a line of hedges; her wheels spun on the grass – and then sank deeply into the soft ground.

The sudden check was too much

for the gallant transatlantic pioneer. She buried her nose in the grass and up came her tail. But Alcock and Brown were unhurt. Forgetting their aching limbs they sprang from the toppled plane to meet the crowd of people rushing towards them. When they announced that they had just flown from Newfoundland Irish jaws dropped in amazement.

Within a few hours the whole world heard the news. Alcock and Brown had crossed the Atlantic in fifteen hours fifty-seven minutes. For this magnificent feat both men were knighted. They also received a £10,000 prize from Lord Northcliffe, the newspaper magnate.

DEVIL DANCE

For several days the pilgrims have been arriving at the *gompa*—the Tibetan name for a monastery. They have toiled up steep mountain slopes with icy winds whipping them; they have plodded patiently through rocky passes between snow-capped peaks. They have endured hardship and danger in a land with few roads so that they can watch special Buddhist lamas perform their religious dances.

When the day comes for the series of dance dramas to begin, the pilgrims wait in a courtyard of the monastery. Suddenly there is a fanfare of trumpets, the boom of gongs, the sound of cymbals and bells, and the strange noise made by Tibetan bagpipes. Into the courtyard comes a procession of grotesque figures. They wear gorgeous costumes and horrific papier mâché masks.

These dance-dramas are like the Miracle Plays of medieval England in that each tells a story which demonstrates a religious truth.

Being Buddhists, the Tibetans believe that people have many lives, which they live one after the other until they finally achieve a state of spiritual perfection. They see this symbolized by a Wheel of Life, and the idea of this wheel is the basis for the ritual dances performed by the lamas.

Tibetan religious dances, which are believed to be older than the ancient Hindu dances of India, rely a great deal on symbolic gestures and dramatic movements. But they are not solemn all the time. To give the spectators a rest from the drama of the dances, there are pauses when masked boys run to the centre of the courtyard and perform comic dances which make the pilgrims roar with laughter.

Tibet, a great plateau surrounded by mountains, and sometimes called the "Roof of the World", is nine times larger than England, yet it has a population of only about two million people.

The Tibetans are probably the most religious people in the world, and every family regards it as a point of honour that at least one of its sons should become a lama, which is the Tibetan equivalent of a monk, or priest.

The most important person in Tibet used to be the Dalai Lama, who lived in a palace on a hill overlooking the capital city of Lhasa. Not only was the Dalai Lama the re-ligious head of the Tibetan people; he also ruled the country like a king.

It was believed that, when the Dalai Lama died, his soul passed into the body of a baby boy born at the same minute. When the baby had been found, he was taken to Lhasa to be trained for his dual role of chief priest and ruler.

One of the annual duties of the Dalai Lama was to be present at a week-long series of dances. These were held in the courtyard of the Dalai Lama's Summer Palace outside Lhasa, and the Dalai Lama watched from a special window. The dancers, who appeared on a special stone stage, were court officials and lamas, and it was regarded as a great honour to perform before the Dalai Lama. By tradition, the dances had to be exactly the same each year, even to the way certain gestures and steps were made.

By nature, Tibetans like to watch a spectacle. They have a word for this, *Te Mo*, which can refer to anything from a performance by a street entertainer to a huge official parade.

Devil Masks

One of the most popular performances of *Te Mo* occurs on the 29th day of the last month in the Tibetan calendar. It is held in a courtyard in the east wing of the Dalai Lama's Potala palace. To the sound of drums and cymbals, a procession of 50 dancers appears. Some wear black hats, with wide brims and banners trailing from them. Others are in the costume and masks of devils.

The aim of this Devil Dance is to drive away evil spirits, and to illustrate religious legends about good deities overcoming and punishing wicked demons. It is a very exciting and boisterous performance and its climax comes when the leading priest takes a cup of wine and throws it over a banner on which is the picture of a demon in boiling oil. At that moment the banner goes up in a great sheet of flame, to everyone's delight.

After this Devil Dance has been performed at the Palace, it is repeated all over Tibet.

Today the Chinese have control of Tibet. The Dalai Lama fled when they took over, and now lives in exile. Under the present circumstances, it is hard to know how much longer the religious customs and dances of the Tibetans will survive.

THE BOY FROM

The two American boys from up country had never been to a town as big as New Orleans in the state of Louisiana before.

They had come from their home town of Springfield, Illinois, in a flatboat with a cargo of corn and live hogs to sell in the big town, and they had come down the Sangamon River into the Illinois River and the great Mississippi.

Now, as they stood before the slave market, a young Negro girl was put up on the platform.

"Run!" the slave traders jeered at the girl. "Run up and down so that we can get a good price for you!"

One of the two watching boys drew his friend away from the scene.

"It's revolting," he said. "If I ever get a chance to hit slavery I'll hit it hard."

The boy who spoke was Abraham Lincoln. In time he was to get his chance to hit slavery. When it came he hit it so hard that he knocked it right out of America.

Abraham Lincoln was born in a log cabin in the wilds of the state of Kentucky and spent all his youth wandering with his family from one log cabin to another.

Sometimes in their travels they only had the stars for a roof. Young Abe rarely had shoes on his feet, and had only a few days schooling in his life.

But people around him soon realized that Abraham Lincoln was more than the ordinary son of a shiftless carpenter. He would cut wood for days to get enough money to buy a book. Many times he would walk a mile just to borrow a grammar book.

When he was offered a job as a shop assistant in a general store the customers always knew where they would find the long, lean body of Abraham Lincoln – curled up on the floor with a book!

Treefeller, carpenter, postmaster, shop assistant, Lincoln was all these before his passion for books led him to study law. He was still in his twenties when he was elected to the Illinois State Legislature – a sort of state parliament.

The question of slavery in America at this time was a vexed one. It was permitted in the southern states; the northern states were by and large opposed to it.

In the North some people organized anti-slavery societies, while other northerners took the view that while slavery was wrong, opposing it would only anger the South.

At first Lincoln belonged to this second group. He considered slavery an evil that should not be allowed to spread outside the southern states.

Lincoln believed that too much interference with the southern slave states would endanger the Union – to which all the states belonged and which really formed America into a whole country. Given time, he thought that slavery would in any case die out in the slave states.

But when Lincoln, always a tremendously popular man, was elected to Congress – the American parliament – and the slavery rift between the North and South widened, he became tougher.

When some opponents of slavery held a meeting to form a new political party – the Republican Party – Lincoln, the boy from the backwoods, went along and made a speech that so moved the audience that even the newspaper reporters were overcome with emotion and were unable to write down a word of it.

After that the cry was, "Lincoln for President!" On November 6, 1860, the votes were counted And Abraham Lincoln set out for the White House.

The southern states knew about Lincoln's views on slavery and became angrier still at his election as President. In the North people feared a civil war.

Even as Lincoln was travelling to the White House news came that the South had set itself up as a new nation, calling itself the Confederacy.

A few weeks later the Confederate army opened fire on the Northern, or Union, forces, and America plunged into civil war.

Two years after the war began President Lincoln decided to fulfil his boyhood promise to hit slavery hard. The weapon he used was a speech freeing all the slaves in the states that had left the Union – in other words, the southern states. It meant that if the North won the war, slavery would end completely in America.

The war's great battle was at the small town of Gettysburg in Pennsylvania: the date, July 1, 1863. Gettysburg was a desperate, terrible battle in which 50,000 men were killed in three violent days.

The North won the day and when

This primitive log cabin was the home of the young Abraham Lincoln.

THE BACKWOODS

General Ulysses Grant won them another great victory at Vicksburg, Mississippi, the North took the battle on to Southern soil.

Meanwhile Lincoln decided to set aside the battlefield of Gettysburg as a national monument. There he went to make the greatest speech ever made by an American: the famous Gettysburg address.

"We here highly resolve that those dead shall not have died in vain – that this nation, under God, shall have a new birth of freedom – and that government of the people, by the people, for the people shall not perish from the earth."

The Northern army chiefs, General Grant and General Sherman, began to plan a great attack on the South. Grant's task was to capture Richmond, the Confederate capital. Sherman was to march an army through Georgia.

Under their two-pronged attack the Confederacy collapsed and four years after the war began, in April 1865, General Lee, the southern commander, surrendered.

A few days later President Lincoln took his wife to the theatre. As they were engrossed in the play an actor named John Wilkes Booth, who was a Confederate sympathizer, threw open the door of their box and shot Lincoln in the head.

Booth was soon cornered and shot dead. He had killed one of the greatest-ever American presidents.

As Lincoln and his wife sat watching a theatre performance, an assassin came into their box and shot him.

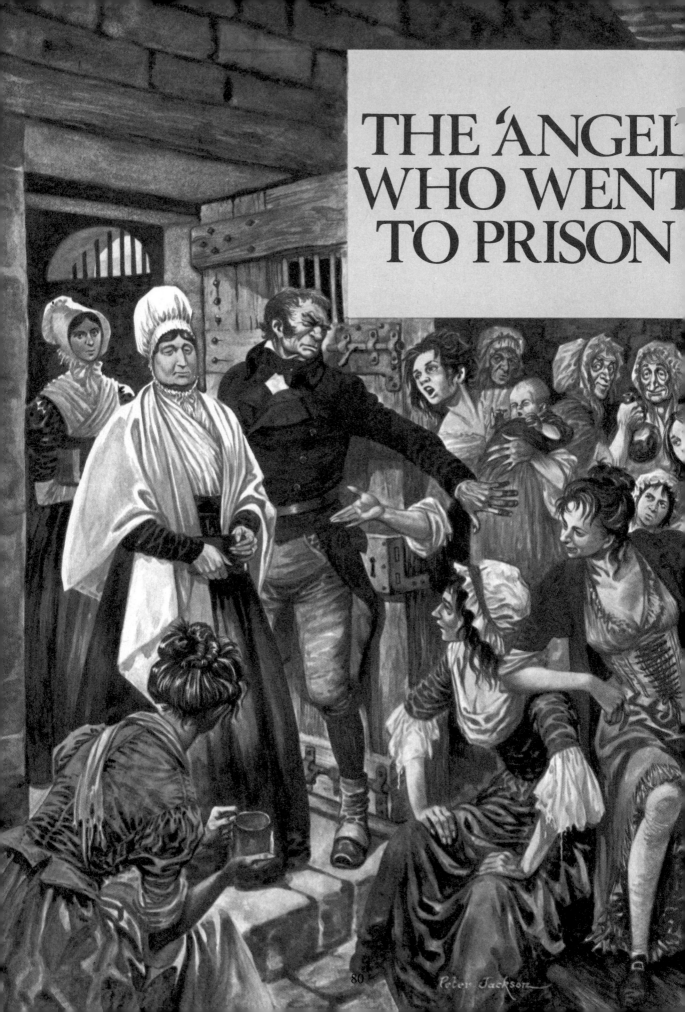

THE 'ANGEL' WHO WENT TO PRISON

Elizabeth Fry was so dismayed by what she saw inside Britain's prisons that she devoted the rest of her life to helping those who were held in such squalid conditions

"R—A—T. . . . Rat," said the teacher at her blackboard.

"Please, Mum, like them ones?" called a boy as he pointed to the rats scurrying in the dark corner of the room.

"*Those* ones. . . . Yes. Like those ones Thomas. Now, say after me. . . ."

Hastily Mrs. Elizabeth Fry turned her face away from the class so they would not see the tear that sprang unbidden to her eye.

For this was no ordinary school. It was nothing more than an empty cell in London's ancient Newgate Prison. The pupils were the children of the prisoners, brought into the prison with their mothers by a blind and outdated legal code.

Born of a wealthy Quaker family who lived outside Norwich, Elizabeth had a taste of London's witty and fashionable society before a sudden revelation drove her back to the country. At nineteen she set up a school for poor children.

Even now her real life's work, the reform of Britain's prisons, had not begun. After her marriage to a strict but wealthy Quaker named Joseph Fry she began to seek out the sick poor of the city and to set up schools and soup kitchens.

Then came the fateful day in 1813 when she visited Newgate Prison.

"Such things must not be!" she cried as she gazed through a double row of bars at the prisoners.

They were more like savage beasts than human beings with their matted hair, their unwashed bodies and their ragged clothes. Begging hands stretched out through the bars to implore charity from the visitors.

Horrible Conditions

And the prisoners needed every bit of charity they could get. Only the barest allowance of food was given – and no clothes. To sleep they huddled on the floor together for warmth with the great prison rats scampering over them.

When Elizabeth spoke with horror to the authorities about the conditions many were actually surprised that she should find anything odd about them.

"Always been like that m'dear young lady," said an old judge. "After all – prison is for punishment you know. . . ."

Elizabeth now understood what she must do. If she could not reform the prisons then she must try to reform the prisoners.

Quite officially, for anyone could visit the prisons – they were quite a favourite "sight" – she set up her school first. The mothers were grateful for her interest in the children and she was able to set to work on them.

She promised to find profitable work for them if they would give up their vices. With their pay they could at last clothe themselves decently.

By now the Governor was co-operating with her.

"Though how she does it I don't know," he confessed, "if I went down in that yard those women would tear me limb from limb."

"You ain't no angel out o' Heaven, sir, begging your pardon," said his senior warder who had already been converted by the grey-eyed Quaker.

At last Elizabeth's work was bearing fruit. The Government set up a committee and Queen Charlotte sent for the Quaker woman to hear at first hand what things were done in her Royal prisons.

With the work of reform in hand in England, Elizabeth Fry went abroad in France, Germany, Denmark, Russia and Switzerland.

Her great career received one visible crown in 1842 – a few years before her death. The King of Prussia, on a visit to England, insisted on going to see her.

"You travelled so many thousands of miles to help the poor people of my prisons," he told her, "that I certainly must return the visit."

THE SAHARA

The Desert That's Full Of Surprises

The Sahara has been described by one writer as "the most beautiful desert of all" – by another as a "fearful void".

Both descriptions are right. For the world's largest hot desert, which has claimed so many lives, offers scenery of breath-taking beauty.

The Sahara extends across North Africa from the Atlantic to the Red Sea, cut only by the Nile. Its width from north to south is 1,600 km or more. Rainfall is so scanty that some parts of it have been known to go for ten years without a drop of rain. It is not surprising that the Arabs named it *sahra* ("wilderness").

The main reason for the lack of rain is that the prevailing wind brings dry continental air from the north-east. Rainfall is not only rare but very irregular. A district may be dry for many months – then suddenly three inches may fall in a few hours.

For a brief period pools appear, and long dried-up water-courses are flooded. Then the water quickly vanishes, soaking into the sand, or evaporated by the hot sun and the dry air.

Thousands of years ago, the region was much cooler and damper. Even in historical times it enjoyed a less arid climate than now. Prehistoric rock carvings and paintings show animals that could not now exist there, and Roman and other remains suggest that there was once a considerable population.

The desert is far from being just a vast sandy plain. There are high mountains – as in the Hoggar (or Ahaggar) and Tibesti highlands. These have peaks rising to over 3,000 metres. Bare rock also appears on the rocky plateaus known as *hammada*, and in small outcrops that rise like islands from the sand.

Much of the rock has been broken up by erosion. Main causes of this are the constant expansion and contraction as the extreme heat by day alternates with acute night-time cold: the action of frost – by no means unknown in the

For the desert nomads the oasis provides much needed water and a chance to rest before setting out, once again, across the seemingly endless sea of sand.

desert; and the abrasive effect of wind and sand.

Rock particles small enough to form sand are carried away by the wind and deposited as ridges, or dunes. The dune areas are known by the term *erg*. Other areas, called *reg*, are covered with small stones and gravel.

In the clear desert light, both dunes and rocks offer fascinating landscapes. The colours of the sand vary from silver grey to rich red-gold, while the rock is often shining black.

Yet to a traveller lost and without water, the bare desert is a pitiless place. After the burning day, night brings little relief, for then it is bitterly cold. Another grim hazard is the sandstorm, reducing visibility to nothing, stinging the face and filling clothes and everything else with gritty particles.

Desert Nomads

Of the sparse population, one of the most interesting peoples are the Tuaregs, many of them Nomads, travelling with their camels and flocks from one area of scanty pasture to another. Their name means "People of the veil", from the blue head-cloth with which they mask their faces.

Settled life occurs only in narrow valleys in mountainous regions, where water exists in sufficient quantities, or in oases. These are found where underground water is near enough to the surface to support vegetation, or to be drawn up from wells.

The most important form of plant life in the oasis is the date palm. It furnishes not only its valuable fruit, but also timber. Its leaves are used for basket-weaving; the date-stones are ground to make feed for camels.

Equally important is the shelter the palms give to smaller trees, such as peach or fig, and to grain crops.

Outside the oases, and the few wadis, or gorges, which contain pools, the only sources of water are scattered water-holes. Often they are no more than a foot or two across, marked by a few stones – easily missed by the thirsty traveller.

Away from the oases, wild animal and plant life is not altogether absent. Where they can reach down to water with their long roots, tough shrubs such as acacia and

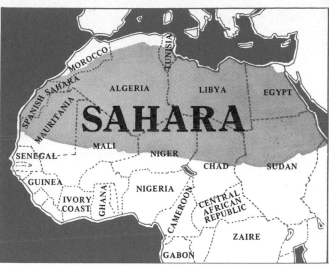

This map shows the area covered by the Sahara desert.

thorny tamarisk stubbornly survive. After a fall of rain, dormant seeds of small plants rapidly germinate, bloom, produce fresh seeds – and just as rapidly die.

On the desert margins, gazelle and fennec (desert fox) live. The strange jerboa, with its tiny forelegs and powerful hindlegs, emerges from its burrow at night to leap in pursuit of food.

Bird life includes the desert lark, crows and bustard, and, in the south, the white-faced scops owl. Horned vipers, lizards and the dangerous scorpion lurk among the rocks.

While camel caravans still make their way across the Sahara, there are now bus and lorry routes running from north to south. Another very important development has been the discovery of valuable minerals, especially oil.

Yet despite the changes the modern world has brought, for many travellers the great desert still holds the magic – and the menace – it has held for so long.

THE FASTEST THING ON TWO WHEELS

1. The history of the motor-cycle, which was to become the fastest thing on two wheels, started in about 1884 when Edward Butler built a tricycle powered by a twin-cylinder engine. In the foreground is an American Copeland steam-bicycle.

2. Motor-cycling was a lonely pastime until 1904 when a seat was provided for a passenger. The large windscreen and flexible body afforded comfortable travelling in this forecar; a forerunner of the sidecar.

3. The first T.T. race was held in the Isle of Man in 1907. It was won by C. R. Collier on a Matchless at an average speed of 38.22 mph. It was a tremendous feat just to complete the course in those early years.

4. Women, too, have had their part in the history of motor-cycling. The Douglas firm made a very successful ladies' model whose riders had to be just as adept at making roadside repairs as their male counterparts.

5. Motor-cycles played a big part in the 1914-18 war. Not only were they used for dispatch carrying, but some were equipped with machine guns mounted on a specially reinforced chassis. These could race swiftly to the battle front.

6. This 1923 Ner-a-car had a two-and-a-half horse power engine. One of its outstanding features was its remarkably good steering. In the background of our picture is a yellow 1922 Wooler, nicknamed the Flying Banana.

7. An ideal means of transport in crowded city streets was this Velocette, which appeared in 1948. It had a water-cooled, twin-cylinder engine and the driving wheel was shaft driven. It was quiet and comfortable to ride.

8. With the coming of the popular motor scooter, more and more people were introduced to the motor-cycle world. In our picture, two scooter enthusiasts watch the riders in a cross-country event on a rough, difficult course.

9. Streamlining has brought increased speed to modern motor-cycles. The T.T. races have helped to develop this for the ordinary motor-cycle and for the faster machines used on the race tracks in the Grand Prix events.

CAMPBELL·THE RECORD

Donald Campbell

It seemed as though the whole of the World's press had sent a representative to the famous motor racing circuit at Goodwood, in Sussex. It was May 1960 and *Bluebird CN7* was about to make its first ever public demonstration. At the wheel of this beautifully streamlined car was speed-king Donald Campbell; son of Sir Malcolm who had six times been holder of the Absolute Water Speed Record with his legendary family of *Bluebird* speedboats.

The new car was the latest creation in a distinguished line of record-breaking cars and boats from the Campbell stable.

The man responsible for designing the *Bluebird CN7* was Kenneth Norris, a brilliant engineer with many years of solid experience behind him. It was Norris who had been responsible for designing Donald Campbell's extremely successful K7 jet-boat, the craft which broke the Water Speed Record more times than any other before or since. Working flat-out with his team of experts, it took Ken Norris no less than 36,000 man-hours in the design stage alone to enable the CN7 to enter the construction phase. A staggering 800 detailed design drawings had to be made, while the jet-boat which had gone before – revolutionary as it was – had only required 8,000 man-hours and 100 drawings. The CN7 was certainly a major undertaking right from the very start.

New Approach

Because he had been instructed by Donald to design a vehicle which would be capable of exceeding 500 m.p.h., Norris chose a radical approach. He opted for a powerful gas-turbine engined layout, utilising a Bristol Proteus powerplant of the type used in the Britannia airliner. The 5,000 horsepower generated by this potent engine was flexible enough to allow the conventional idea of a gearchange mechanism to be dispensed with altogether. In order to achieve greater stability during the fierce period of acceleration preceeding the measured mile, the new *Bluebird* featured four-wheel drive and Dunlop tyres of extremely large diameter.

In order to test the main structure of *Bluebird* the car was hoisted 6 metres above the ground and then dropped.

BREAKER

A special underground testing plant had to be built, at a cost of some £125,000, in order to test the performance of these purpose-designed tyres and to ensure that there would be no risk of them bursting at high speeds. Various tyres were made for different stages in the CN7's development programme; some tyres were built with a 350 m.p.h. speed limit for the early test runs, whilst stronger constructions were to be used for the actual record attempt.

Super Strength

Bluebird's main body structure was an absolute masterpiece of engineering. By sandwiching together various layers of strong, yet light, metal skins, then bonding them under pressure with special high-temperature adhesives, the skilled engineers responsible for constructing the main body-shell managed to combine low overall weight with very high structural strength. A spectacular sight during the course of this construction programme came when the manufacturers decided to test the strength of the main structure by dropping it from a height of six metres onto a concrete floor! To the obvious delight – not to mention relief – of the assembled experts, the *Bluebird* held fast.

Naturally enough, once a high-speed vehicle has reached its maximum speed, the question arises as to the quickest method of slowing it down again before running out of track at the end of the course. The *Bluebird CN7* had a special parachute which would slow the car from top speed down to around 250 m.p.h. The CN7 also sported a pair of huge air-brakes which flipped out into the airflow from the car's streamlined flanks and assisted in reducing the car's speed still further. No less than eighty UK-based engineering companies participated in this mammoth construction programme and the car, which was reported to have cost over £1 million to build, absorbed a further £1

Campbell's keeness to make *Bluebird* a record-breaker was to lead to disaster. Whilst on a test run the car went out of control and crashed.

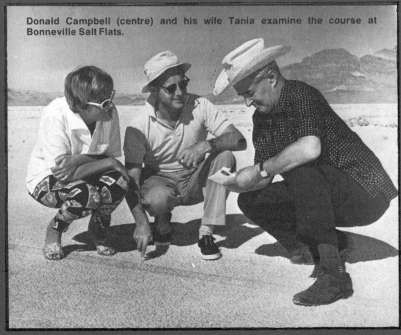

Donald Campbell (centre) and his wife Tania examine the course at Bonneville Salt Flats.

million in its four year life-span as an active record-breaker.

Once the lengthy task of construction had been completed, *Bluebird* was rolled out for that first public demonstration at Goodwood, before being crated up and shipped to the United States for Donald Campbell's first crack at the World Land Speed Record.

On arrival at the Bonneville Salt Flats, which was to be the venue for this maiden record attempt, the *Bluebird* team set about the tough and time-consuming job of carrying out the many preliminary test runs. It is a sobering thought that *Bluebird's* minimum speed, with no throttle on at all, was over 180 m.p.h.!

At 6 a.m. on 16 September 1960, Donald Campbell set off on his fifth timed trial run. The tyres fitted that day had a 300 m.p.h. test limit, but Donald in his keen enthusiasm got carried away, and he was doing 360 m.p.h. before he had time to check his speedometer and take correcting action. In a terrible instant, *Bluebird* snapped to the left, shot into the air and somersaulted over and over in a ghostly cloud of salt spray and pale blue paint.

When the dust finally settled, the support team rushed to the scene of the accident. Pieces of blue-painted wreckage were strewn all over the place, and a trail of blood from the *Bluebird's* cockpit led everyone to expect the worst. When chief mechanic Leo Villa prised open the cockpit cover, a wave of relief swept the whole British team. Donald was alive. He lay semi-conscious in the twisted remains of what was once his pride and joy, and amazed everyone by having the presence of mind to switch off the *Bluebird's* Proteus gas-turbine engine which, surprisingly, was still ticking over after the violent battering it had just endured.

In the intensive-care ward of the hospital in nearby Wendover, Donald's injuries were announced to the anxiously waiting pressmen. His skull was fractured, an eardrum had been pierced, and he was suffering from severe cuts, bruises and concussion. A reporter stooped by Campbell's bedside and asked what his next course of action would be. "I'm going to have another try," was the brave Englishman's terse reply.

It is almost impossible for us to even begin to understand the degree of courage and sheer will-power exhibited by Donald Campbell during his recovery to full record-breaking health after his fearful accident.

Small Changes

Bluebird CN7 had to be virtually rebuilt. Only the engine unit and the immensely strong cockpit section were saved from the original construction. A tall vertical tail-fin was fitted for improved stability at high speeds, and numerous other small modifications made to various other parts of the car in order to ensure maximum performance potential for the next attempt on the World Land Speed Record.

The rebuilding of the car was completed by November 1961, but the actual venue for Donald's next try was far from decided. The salt surface at Bonneville had degenerated considerably, and Donald – who was a very superstitious character at the best of times – felt that Bonneville held a jinx for him and wanted to find a fresh speed-track. As things turned out, Campbell could hardly have chosen a more unlucky place. He opted for Lake Eyre, South Australia; a dried-up brine lake of vast proportions.

It was not until the spring of 1963 that the Campbell entourage finally got *Bluebird* and all its support equipment and spares out to Lake Eyre. Then there began an epic struggle against the almost totally unpredictable Australian weather conditions.

Just as the *Bluebird* team was

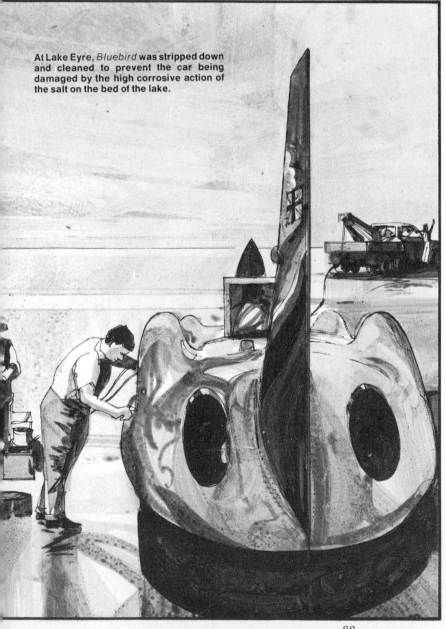

At Lake Eyre, *Bluebird* was stripped down and cleaned to prevent the car being damaged by the high corrosive action of the salt on the bed of the lake.

getting ready for the expedition into the centre of Lake Eyre, the skies opened up and it simply poured down for weeks and weeks. The entire area around Lake Eyre became flooded to waist-level. One morning, the already-demoralised team awoke to find all their precious crates of spare parts floating in 1.5 metres of water. Another time, the four-ton *Bluebird* almost cracked the deteriorating salt surface of the lake. Fortunately, Campbell and his crew managed to tow the car clear with the use of a half-a-dozen Land Rovers equipped with heavy-duty winching gear.

Return Home

Their luck held out in this respect, but due to disagreements within the team's personnel it was decided to abandon the attempt and return to England.

Despite the difficulties and set-backs which had gone before, the *Bluebird* team resolved to make one final attempt at the record and reassembled at their Australian base at Muloorina in April 1964 to try again. Back home in England, Campbell had managed to whip up some additional sponsorship money from a group of patriotic United Kingdom based companies.

It was not good news which greeted the *Bluebird* team on their return to Lake Eyre. Heavy rains were forecast for the following week, just when Donald planned to have a crack at the record. Embittered by their bad fortune, Campbell and his crew pressed on with their preparations.

The rain fell yet again and waterlogged one end of the specially-flattened course. Donald had thus lost two miles of the accelerating distance, not to mention the vital leeway required for safe braking at the end of each run.

Finally, on 17 July 1964, Campbell set out on his last desperate attempt. As history now records Donald and *Bluebird* made it at last – their speed was 403.10 m.p.h. Courage and perseverance had paid off in the end.

The moment he was discharged from hospital Campbell went straight back to the job of getting *Bluebird* ready for another attempt at the Land Speed Record.

Triumph at last for Campbell and his team as *Bluebird* smashes the Land Speed Record.

The Empress Josephine.

The Sad Empress

When Napoleon returned from Egypt, he and Josephine became involved in a fierce qua[...]

From the moment that Napoleon Bonaparte married Josephine Beauharnais he began to win battles.

In her early teens the girl from the sugar island of Martinique had come to France for an arranged marriage with a young aristocrat, Vicompte Alexandre de Beauharnais. She hoped that she would like her hitherto unseen husband, but he despised, bullied and neglected her. Five years later, Josephine, now the mother of two small children, gladly agreed to a separation.

A long holiday in Martinique was interrupted when news of the Revolution sent Josephine hurrying back to her son, at school in Paris. At first she was safe, but matters grew worse and everyone with a title was viewed with suspicion. Many were imprisoned and many guillotined. Alexandre de Beauharnais was amongst these latter: Josephine almost followed him, but was saved by the timely death of Robespierre, leader of the Terror.

The Terror over, the French people became almost hysterically intent upon pleasure, and during this strange interlude Josephine met the up-and-coming General Bonaparte. He fell in love with her immediately, but she was not impressed at first by the strange young man with the intent stare and untidy clothes.

However, she allowed herself to be persuaded, and became Citizeness Bonaparte. Her new husband had to leave almost at once for Italy, to command the army of the Republic. Josephine resumed her rather frivolous life in Paris, with the difference that she was now bombarded with letters urging her to join Napoleon in Italy. But Josephine was enjoying her popularity among the Parisians, who knew that her husband was responsible for the army's victories.

At last she made the difficult journey to Italy. Josephine's gentle sweetness appealed to everyone save the Bonaparte family, rough, proud people who found the polished Parisian shallow, affected – and possessing far too much influence over their powerful brother.

They all returned to France but Napoleon was soon off again, this time to Egypt. Josephine could deal with trouble-makers on the spot, but she feared that ill-wishers on Napoleon's staff were slandering her behind her back. She was quite correct! On his return the couple had a terrible quarrel, but in the end they made it up, to the chagrin of the other Bonapartes.

Napoleon now made himself dictator, by a show of armed force, and soon afterwards changed his title of First Consul to that of Emperor. This sparked off shattering quarrels amongst the Bonaparte clan, all of whom wished to be transformed into royalty.

At the Coronation of Napoleon Bonaparte, in 1804, it was the Emperor himself who placed the crown upon his wife's head.

The Coronation was a splendid affair. Napoleon, once so shabby, appeared in velvet, ermine and gold while Josephine was dressed in white and wearing priceless diamonds. She knelt before her husband as he placed the crown upon her beautiful chestnut hair.

Josephine as Empress now set the fashion with delicate gowns of silk and muslin, exquisite classical jewellery. She spent enormous sums on clothes, had literally hundreds of dresses, and like less distinguished people, often hesitated to reveal all her debts.

She tried hard to generate a friendly atmosphere at Napoleon's formal court. "Why is it that people don't seem to enjoy themselves?" asked the Emperor plaintively, not realising how much they were in awe of him.

The pair had no children and this increasingly worried them. Josephine had a son and daughter by her first marriage, Eugene and Hortense Beauharnais, and Josephine had

performed one of her few selfish acts by persuading Hortense to marry Napoleon's younger brother Louis. She hoped that Napoleon would be willing to adopt their children as his heirs. In spite of three little sons Hortense's married life was unhappy, and the Emperor still hankered after a child of his own. He decided to divorce Josephine and marry a younger woman.

Disastrous Campaign

The Empress was heartbroken, for she had come to love Napoleon deeply. Nevertheless the divorce went through and later Napoleon married the Austrian princess, Marie Louise. The purpose of this second contract was fulfilled when a son was born. The baby was barely toddling when his father embarked upon a campaign against Russia. But Napoleon's Russian venture proved disastrous. The French did not realise how

disastrous until the remnants of the once proud Grand Army stumbled home with frostbitten limbs after their terrible winter trek across Russia.

During the next year Josephine lived through a nightmare. The Empire was in ruins with common soldiers and Marshals alike deserting their posts. Josephine's son, Eugene, was pressed to change sides in the name of his father-in-law, the king of Bavaria, but his reaction was of the kind that rarely dignifies the pages of history. "I know that the King of Bavaria would rather have an honest private man as his son-in-law than a traitor, however highly placed", and he remained loyal to the fallen Napoleon.

The Russian Tsar visited Josephine at Malmaison, and fearful for the fate of her family, she set herself to win his protection for them. But she became ill with a throat infection. Within a few days she was gravely ill, and died whilst Napoleon, unaware of her fate, was exiled upon Elba.

ENGLAND can often beat the Australians in Test cricket but rarely can we claim to *rout* them. They breed them stubborn down under and only occasionally does England produce the bowler (or pair of bowlers) who can really break their hearts and backs right down to No. 11.

To capture 30-plus wickets in a five-match rubber is not an easy task in games involving cricket's oldest international rivals. The great Sussex bowler Maurice Tate took 38 wickets in the 1924–25 series in Australia and it was not until 1953 that Surrey's Alec Bedser improved the record by one.

When the Bedser figure was overtaken three years later it was not bettered by a mere one or two wickets. It crashed, as did a number of other bowling records, in sensational fashion to the off-spin bowling of a Surrey-based Yorkshireman, Jim Laker, who to the younger generation of cricket followers is the cool, calm commentator for today's TV viewers.

At the time it was difficult to believe one bowler – and a spin bowler at that – could on separate occasions take all 10 Australian wickets in an innings and in one Test match capture all but one of the wickets. Today, in the record books, his 46 Test wickets in that wet 1956 summer often read as misprints. But it did happen . . .

Laker will go down in cricket history as one of the greatest off-spin bowlers of all time. On sticky or dusty wickets he was often unplayable and once in a Test trial returned 8 wickets for 2 runs in 14 overs.

He formed an outstanding spin-bowling partnership for Surrey and England with Tony Lock. Together they helped their county win the championship for seven successive years from 1952–58 but in 1956 it was Laker who stole most of the headlines when he found himself bowling to the Australian side, captained by Ian Johnson.

There is little doubt that the Australian party arrived with their tails down and the long-term weather forecasts were not good for their hopes of regaining the Ashes. They needed firm wickets but instead had one of England's worst summers for rain.

Jim Laker created Test Match history and wrote his name in the record books as his almost unplayable spin bowling put paid to the bemused Australian batsmen.

TEST MATCH TRIUMPH

Their troubles started in the middle of May when they faced Surrey, then at the peak of their championship-winning run, at The Oval. After a good opening stand of 62, one by one they fell victims of Laker's nagging accuracy. In a spell of 46 overs, Laker took all 10 wickets for 88 runs.

The Australian captain tried the same bowling tactics when Surrey batted. After just three overs with his fast bowlers, he relied on spin throughout while Surrey piled up a first innings lead of almost 100. As if they had not seen enough of him already, Laker at No. 6, hammered 16 in one over and scored 43.

Again in the second innings, the Australians made a good start only to collapse to spin again. They slumped from 56-0 to 107 all out with Lock this time taking seven wickets and Laker another two. For the first time in over 40 years a touring Australian team had lost to a county side.

There is little doubt that Laker did more than just take all 10 wickets in that match. He badly damaged the Australian morale and they had to wait until the weather improved in mid-June before showing any sort of form.

They gained a much overdue victory in the second Test at Lord's – the first Test was a draw – and seemed set to go two-up in the series at Leeds after England had lost three quick wickets on the first morning. A century by England captain Peter May helped England recover and then Laker and Lock twice bowled the Australians out for less than 150 for England to square the series with two Tests to play.

As holders of the Ashes, England needed to win just one of the remaining games and this they did in the Fourth Test at Manchester in one of the most amazing clashes between the two countries.

Before the game England caused something of a sensation by naming the semi-retired Rev. David Sheppard, of Sussex, in the side. Two years earlier Sheppard had captained England against Pakistan but he gave up regular first-class cricket to enter the church. When his Test recall came he had played only four innings for Sussex that season – scoring 97 in one of them against the Australians.

Like the earlier selection of Cyril Washbrook for the Third Test, the selectors were proved right when Sheppard, always a good player of fast bowling, scored 113 and helped England run up a big total.

As early as the first day there were questions being asked about the state of the Old Trafford pitch and as the England total mounted up, the tourists eyed it suspiciously. Obviously they did not relish the thought of batting last against the England spinners.

If it did begin to break up on the second day, the England tail made light work of facing the Australian spin attack of Johnson and Benaud. Sheppard went comfortably to his century and in a cheeky half an hour Godfrey Evans hit a brisk 47.

Facing an England total of 459 there was no sign of the drama to come as Colin McDonald and Jim Burke began Australia's reply just after 2.30 p.m. on that amazing Friday, July 27.

The total had moved to 48 without loss when the England captain May made the decision which was to bring about Laker's dream day. He decided to switch his

Ten wickets for 53 runs! It seemed impossible, yet that was the incredible achievement of England's Jim Laker.

trump cards, Laker and Lock, to opposite ends and with his seventh ball from the Stretford end Laker had McDonald caught in his leg trap. This was just the first of 19 wickets Laker was to take from that end during the match.

Four balls later he produced an unplayable ball to the left-hander Neil Harvey and bowled him. The rout had started – 48 for 2.

At tea the Australians, although not badly placed at 62 for 2, were obviously convinced the wicket had gone and that Laker was impossible to tame. Less than 40 minutes later they were all out for 84 in one of the most dramatic collapses in Test history. Laker's figures were 16.4 overs, 4 maidens, 37 runs and 9 wickets. In 22 balls after tea he had taken seven wickets for eight runs.

Forced To Retire

Worse was to come when the Australian followed on, 375 runs behind. Again Burke and McDonald played confidently until McDonald was forced to retire hurt with an injured knee.

This brought in Harvey and amazingly in the crisis he hit his first ball – a full toss from Laker – straight into the hands of mid-wicket. England could hardly believe their luck – the great Harvey dismissed for two ducks – and on the same day at that.

The Australians survived any further disasters that day and with rain reducing play on the Saturday and Monday to a little under two hours for the loss of one more wicket to Laker, it did seem possible that they could save the game.

At lunch on the fifth and last day, McDonald and Craig

had taken the score past 100 without further loss and very few balls had beaten the bat.

Suddenly the sun came out and the wicket began to dry. It was Laker's end again where the vital breakthrough came when he trapped Craig l.b.w. Ten runs later, at 124, Mackay was caught – again off Laker. Miller and Archer followed as the tireless McDonald batted on. But he was fast running out of partners.

Still there at tea, after batting over five hours spread over four days, it seemed McDonald could still save the game for Australia. But Laker had the final word just after tea when the stubborn McDonald fell another victim to Laker's leg trap.

The end was now in sight. Seven wickets down and all to Laker. Could he perform the seemingly impossible feat of taking all 10 Australian wickets for the second time in a season?

With Lock continually beating the bat at the other end, it was obvious he was not out to leave it all to his Surrey partner. But Laker took his eighth and ninth wickets and as the clock neared 5.30 he appealed for l.b.w. against Maddocks. Up went the umpire's finger and the impossible had been achieved – all 10 wickets for 53; 19 wickets in the match.

Although it will go down in cricket history as Laker's match, the Australians did much to contribute to their troubles by poor batting. In all during that eventful season they faced Laker seven times and lost 63 wickets to his biting spin.

Throughout the whole season Laker took 132 wickets – which illustrates clearly how it is possible for one bowler to dominate his opponents.

Hard-Hitting Horsemen

Three young officers of the 10th Hussars were sitting in a tent at Aldershot in the year 1869. They were bored. Lunch was over and the three, were reading newspapers to pass the time. Then one of them spotted an article in *The Field* magazine, about a game played by the Manipuris of India.

"By Jove! It must be a goodish game. I vote we try it." said another and so they mounted their horses, found some long crooked sticks and a billiard ball, and started to play. This, as one of the young men later described it, was how the game of polo was reintroduced into Western Europe after a lapse of many centuries.

Polo was invented in Asia, in an area where every man and boy rode a horse – perhaps in Iran, Central Asia, China or India. The Sassanian Persians, whose cavalry so often ran rings around the Romans, played *chupaan* on horseback with a ball and racket. This was probably similar to the medieval Persians' *chaugan* which was certainly a simple, if rather rough, version of polo. Some ancient poems describe mighty Turkish princes striking the polo-ball "over the moon" or "into the clouds". More down to earth was the true story of Harun al Rashid, that Caliph of Baghdad who appears in so many Arabian Nights fairy tales. He,

playing the game as a child, was too small to reach the ball with his polo stick.

Even though played by Caliphs, polo was regarded by some pompous people as a disreputable pastime. Ahmad Hassan, a Wazir, or prime-minister, of the young prince of Ghazna in 1030 AD, put it in the same class as fighting, drinking and being undignified in public!

Nevertheless polo remained popular with the famed cavalrymen of Islam, particularly among those Saracens and Mamluks who eventually drove the Crusaders from the Holy Land. Not that their foes weren't eager to learn. The Byzantine Greeks played a version of polo though with a softer ball.

One way or another primitive polo spread far and wide, even to Wales where during the reign of Elizabeth I *knappan* was played by men both riding and on foot. Unfortunately, over a thousand people often joined in one game, and the fights that developed got so bad that Welsh *knappan* had to be banned!

Although those three young gentlemen of the 10th Hussars actually introduced polo to England, their comrades fighting for the

British Empire in India already played the game. They called it polo from the Tibetan word *pulu* which meant a ball made from willow wood. It was still disorganized and had very few rules. But the British were determined to introduce discipline and make polo a more orderly pastime. This was done by the high-class Hurlingham Club in 1872.

At first played with five riders per team, and later with only four, polo rapidly became popular in Britain, the USA, Europe and Latin America. The first international match between Britain and the States was played in 1886. Britain won.

In this country polo remained an expensive game for the well-off but in the Americas, north and south, it not surprisingly caught on among the ranch-hands. Country-polo, as it was called, was played in the American West on oiled, grassless fields, while in Argentina it almost grew into a national sport. Perhaps polo has gone back to what it was in the beginning – a tough game for men who live and work on horseback, whether they be American cowboys, Argentinian gauchos, nomadic tribesmen from Central Asia or the Saracen cavalry of Saladin.

THE DORMOUSE'S LONG SLEEP

With its large prominent black eyes, pink ears, golden brown back and flanks and creamy white underparts, the common dormouse is one of Britains most attractive small mammals, both in appearance and habits. The head and body of an adult measures 63.5 to 89 mm, and the thickly-furred tail is almost the same length.

Mainly nocturnal, the dormouse spends the daylight hours curled up asleep in a nest, usually above the ground in a thick bush, and is seldom seen unless disturbed when, after pausing to sleepily look around and to twitch its fine long black whiskers, it displays speed and agility in making an escape, threading a way through tangled brambles with consumate ease.

The nest itself is a loose ball, about 100 mm. in diameter, woven from dried grass-stems, leaves and honeysuckle bark and although they are seldom well hidden they can be most difficult to find; thick masses of bramble, honeysuckle and blackthorn are favourite sites.

At dusk the dormouse emerges from its nest to search for wild fruits, nuts and berries, this diet being supplemented by young leaves, honeysuckle bark and sometimes small insects. Dormice have been known to steal birds eggs, but on the whole they are harmless little creatures.

For breeding, a larger nest 150 to 175 mm. in diameter is constructed and lined with soft material such as hair, wool or thistle-down.

Litters of two to seven, usually three, are born after a gestation period of 21 to 24 days. Blind and almost naked at birth, the young acquire a covering of fur after thirteen or fourteen days and their eyes open four days later.

In a little over four weeks they will venture out of the nest becoming independent when about six weeks old and sexually mature after about twelve months. Two possibly three litters a year are produced and autumn births are not unusual, although these late season young have little chance of putting on sufficient fat to see them through the winter.

Sometimes locally known as the "seven sleepers" (months) dormice are true hibernators. In late September or early October, having acquired a thick layer of subcutaneous fat, they retire individually to a hibernaculum, or winter nest, usually in a hollow tree or tucked away in the base of a hazel bush.

There, rolled up into a ball, with eyes and mouth tightly closed, head bent, ears folded flat against the head and tail folded under the body and over the head, the dormouse slips into hibernation. So deep is this sleep that the creature may be gently lifted from its nest without disturbance. Depending on the weather hibernation can last until the following May by which time these delightful little creatures will have lost almost half their autumn weight.

The distribution of the dormouse is confined to the South of England and Wales.

RACE OF A THOUSAND CORNERS

Alberto Ascari, brilliant son of a great Italian driver, Antonio Ascari who had been killed 30 years before, began the Monaco Grand Prix on May 22, 1955, determined to regain the title of world champion which he had held in 1952 and 1953 but lost in 1954 to the Brazilian Juan Fangio.

Driving a Lancia he equalled Fangio's best time in practice, and both men shared the leading positions on the starting grid with Britain's Stirling Moss who, like Fangio, was driving a Mercedes.

But the "Race of a Thousand Corners" as Monaco is called, is a terrible strain on both driver and car. Halfway through the 100 laps of the twisting three kilometre circuit, Fangio lost the lead to Moss and retired when the transmission on his car broke.

Ascari moved up into second place and was desperately chasing Moss when, with only 20 laps to go, the British driver also had to pull into the pits with the blue smoke of burning oil pouring from his engine.

But Ascari did not know this – all he knew was that by making up one second a lap he could overhaul Moss and he came roaring out of the tunnel and drove his big red car towards the harbour chicane at a furious pace, determined to do just that.

But he miscalculated the vital corner and the car shot through the straw bales, missing an iron bollard by a

98

fraction, and, with Ascari still clutching the wheel, smashed into the water and sank, bubbling furiously, to the muddy harbour bottom.

A rescue boat was soon on the scene, but before frogmen could dive overboard, Ascari's "lucky" blue helmet, which he always wore, broke the surface and the dripping driver was hauled on board. All he had suffered – apart from a blow to his pride – was a broken nose.

Ascari was one of the more superstitious of the racing drivers of his day and, for those who believe in such things, it was astonishing that he ignored the implications of his lucky escape in the 13th running of the Monaco Grand Prix.

Four days later, a month exactly before the 30th anniversary of his father's death, Ascari, apart from his injured nose, none-the-worse – or wiser – for his miraculous escape, was at the Monza track near to his Italian home.

Although he did not have his lucky blue helmet with him, on the spur of the moment he decided to try a new Ferrari sports car belonging to a friend. For some unknown reason the car skidded at high speed, crashed and Ascari was killed.

His father had also had a "lucky" helmet and it was while driving for the first time without it he also had died.

Monaco is unique because it is the last of the Grand Prix races for Formula 1 cars to be run on public roads. It is also the smallest of the circuits and the one with the most corners. Drivers estimate that well over 2,000 gear changes have to be made during the race.

The course goes past such famous Monte Carlo tourist attractions as the Hotel de Paris, the Casino and, of course, the harbour packed with millionaires' yachts and motor boats.

The corners, the curbs and the continual overtaking on the small circuit make it a race notorious for sorting out the men from the boys. A single patch of oil on the narrow streets can cause a multiple pile-up.

Five cars smashed into each other in the 1932 race and 20 years later half the field had to retire on the very first lap after colliding on the promenade.

A driver named Fagioli was one of those who "preferred" to hit the promenade wall rather than go into the sea. He did it once, and escaped unhurt. Fifteen years later he crashed again at exactly the same spot – and was killed.

A coincidence at Monaco also brought one of his wittiest remarks from that great British driver Graham Hill. He made his Grand Prix debut at Monaco – and a wheel fell off his car.

Many years later, Graham, who won Monaco five times, drove in his hundredth Grand Prix there – and again lost a wheel. "At least you can't say I'm not consistent on this circuit," he commented.

The Monaco Grand Prix circuit runs through the streets of the city itself. The drivers have to change gear over 2,000 times during the race because of the number of corners on the circuit.

THE WILY FOX

There is a story of three old dog foxes which, when the huntsmen were out, would take it in turns to lead the hounds a dance. When the first was tired, he would lead the pack to the second fox, who would take up the game until, weary, he would lead the hounds to the third, and so on.

That tale sounds almost too amazing to be true, but if any creature is capable of devising such a trick, then it is the wily fox. Aesop's fables depict the fox as a cunning creature, and this is certainly true.

Foxes grow more wily as they age, and a hunted fox will try all sorts of things to throw the hounds off the scent, such as running through a herd of cattle, or along the tops of narrow walls, making it difficult for the hounds to follow.

And the fox needs to be wily, if it is to survive at all! For it has angered so many farmers and poultry-owners by its raids on lambs and chickens that it is known as a public enemy.

The spread of towns and the increased amount of broiler-house poultry-farming has deprived the fox of farmyard chickens and made life harder for him.

Favourite Food

But now that rabbits, once decimated by the myxomatosis purge, have returned in vast numbers to the fields of Britain, the fox could be the farmer's friend. It is not often tempted to attack stock, apart from poultry and the occasional lamb. The main part of its diet consists of beetles, small birds, berries, mice and hedgehogs, for it is quite a small creature itself.

Apart from the red fox, there is the arctic fox and the grey fox.

If it had not been for the musk glands of the fox, and the resulting very strong smell, the red fox would have made a wonderful domestic animal, especially as a pet, because it is exceptionally intelligent.

In the wild the fox has an easier time to some extent. There it does not tread on the toes of civilised man, though it has to face the natural hazards of life in the wild, including the threat of fire. But at least in the real wilds the hunting horn will not spell danger. Wherever it lives it never ceases to be clever. The saying, "as cunning as a fox," is no exaggeration.

Small birds, berries, mice and hedgehogs are all part of the hungry fox's diet.

THE LIONHEART'S PRISON

THE iron-bound door creaked open and the new prisoner was escorted into the gloomy dungeon. Curiously he glanced at the row of guards standing to attention against the reddish stone walls, the smoky light of their torches glinting on their drawn swords.

He could tell that the guards had been specially chosen. Indeed, if he were to escape they would have to answer with their lives because he was the most valuable prisoner in the world. And it was no coincidence that of all the available castles, he had been sent to the grim Castle Trifels. Usually it was reserved for desperate traitors, and it was said that few prisoners ever left its dank dungeons alive. But this prisoner, who had to be guarded with drawn swords, was no common traitor – he was Richard Coeur de Lion of England.

No country is as famous for its castles as Germany. To the traveller it seems that wherever there is a good

An aerial view of Trifels in about the year 1400. The castle is one of the most successful of the Hohenstaufen (imperial fortress) group, in which the combination of defence, decoration and size are seen to best advantage. Trifels is one of the famous "Trinity of Fortresses", all of which are situated on rocky heights.

DAN ESCLOTT

vantage point there is the ruin of a fortress on it. This is because Germany was late to become a unified country. Prior to this the land was governed by many local rulers, each with his own castle.

In the Pfalzerwald, which is the largest single forest in Germany situated in the Rhineland Palatinate, there are ruins of no less than four hundred fortresses. The most outstanding of these is the Castle Trifels which stands on a towering peak overlooking the town of Annweiler. It is of particular interest to British visitors because it was here that King Richard was imprisoned.

King Richard, born in 1157, was really more interested in adventuring in Palestine than in governing England. In 1187 the great Saracen leader Saladin had captured Jerusalem from the Christians. Two years later, after his coronation, King Richard began to plan a crusade to recapture the city and make it safe for Christian pilgrims who wished to visit the Holy Sepulchre there. As he was short of money, the King sold off many of his English castles to finance the expedition.

In 1191 he set off with 4,000 men-at-arms and 4,000 foot soldiers in a hundred transports. In the Holy Land he was very popular with his troops on account of his personal courage. During the siege of Acre he was badly stricken with fever. Unable to walk, he ordered his servants to carry him out on a litter so that, propped up on silk cushions, he was able to fire his crossbow at the enemy.

But he was not popular with his European allies whom he despised because he felt that they were not doing enough for the Crusade. He offended most of them and as a result did not get enough support to capture Jerusalem. He did get within a few miles of the city, and here he

Knowing that escape from Trifels was virtually impossible, Richard the Lionheart settled down to lead as comfortable a life as possible. But he believed that help was forthcoming and that proved to be the case. Just over a year after being taken prisoner he was returned to England.

The castle of Trifels as it appears today. The stump of the tower remains and part of the palace has been reconstructed.

made a truce with Saladin who promised to allow Christian pilgrims to visit the shrines in safety.

On October 9th, 1192, Richard set sail for England, but being delayed by storms, he decided to travel on foot through the territory of Leopold of Austria. He disguised himself for the journey but, on December 16th, he was arrested near Vienna dressed as a kitchen servant.

On March 23rd the next year he was delivered to the Emperor, Henry VI, at Speyer, where he was charged with various crimes (including the betrayal of the Holy Land to Saladin), and a colossal ransom of 150,000 marks was placed on him.

At first the Emperor Henry VI treated him as an honoured guest because of his kingly rank, but later he sent Richard to Trifels where there was little chance of rescue or escape.

The grim dungeon of the castle and the fierce guards did not depress the English King. Soon he challenged the guards one by one to wrestling matches in which he always managed to win. He also gained their admiration and friendship by spending the evenings proving that he could drink more wine than they. As he was paying for the wine, the guards enjoyed these contests more than the wrestling.

One legend tells that the whereabouts of the King were found by one of his followers who sang a song under the walls of the castle. It was the King's favourite song, and he

sang it back thus letting his friend know that he was captive there.

Whether this is true or just a tale is not known, but King Richard's friend Longchamp did intercede with the German Emperor and managed to get him removed from Trifels to better quarters at Hagenau before he was returned to England in March, 1194.

The origins of Trifels go back into the time of legend. It is known that it was an Imperial residence in the 12th and 13th centuries when the Emperor's crown and treasure were kept there. The castle is built of massive red stones which are the same colour as the pinnacle on which it stands, so that it gives an impression of being part of the living rock. No road reaches it. The visitor has to toil up a steep track for nearly half an hour to reach its gateway. Below Annweiler looks like a tiny model town while the Pfalzerwald stretches from horizon to horizon like a great green sea.

No wonder it was regarded as impregnable being built on the top of such a steep crag.

There is a legend that Trifels once housed the Holy Grail, the mystical chalice which had held the blood of Christ and which King Arthur and his Knights of the Round Table were always seeking.

In 1937 much of Trifels was restored to give an idea of what the castle must have been like in its heyday, with huge cool halls and cloisters. Today in the Great Hall symphony concerts are sometimes held and Shakespearean plays produced against an authentic castle setting.

One of the most colourful of Britain's birds is the goldfinch.

The common gull is a winter visitor to Britain and despite its name is less commonly seen than many other gulls.

You can often see the magpie, a member of the crow family, when walking through woodlands.

OUT ABOUT FEATHERS

If you are looking for a hobby which is both interesting and cheap why not start collecting birds' feathers. Your specimens, picked up in the woods and parks, will cost you nothing.

You will need an album to keep your feathers in. Each one should be fastened with a small piece of transparent sticky tape and the details of the bird it came from written clearly by the side of it. It is essential to have a good book about birds with plenty of pictures in it to help you identify your finds. If you cannot afford to buy a book then go to your local library and borrow one.

Birds constantly lose their feathers, so there are always plenty to be found on country walks and in parks. Take a large envelope to carry the feathers in and make sure that you keep them as flat as possible until you are able to put them in your album.

This colourful bird is the pied woodpecker. It feeds on insects and makes its home in woodlands and parks.

Below; the jay is a colourful member of the crow family.

You may often see this bird hanging upside down. It is a great tit and is well known for its acrobatic antics.

Dubrovnik's port, viewed from the ramparts.

EVERYONE LOVES DUBROVNIK

E veryone loves Dubrovnik. Yugoslavia's Adriatic jewel is now a tourist paradise, and in high summer all the languages of Europe babble away in the Stradone, the long, elegantly-paved street that bisects the town.

The tourists come mainly for the big hotels along the coast and when the sun goes down they make their way into the old city, with its shops and restaurants. What they find is not just another old city, the nub of a tourist trap, but one that is encircled by a massive and magnificent wall.

"Protectors' or visitors, they come from all over the world to this Yugoslavian city

The wall has two great towers and on its landward side is reinforced with a moat. From the wall, reached by stairways, there is a splendid view of the town's pink roof tiles, its towers and the blue Adriatic beyond. It is almost impossible to imagine anyone capturing Dubrovnik against such a formidable obstacle.

In fact, Dubrovnik has usually been a pawn used by neighbouring states to bargain with, rather than a place to lay siege to. It was called Ragusa when its famous wall was built in the thirteenth century, and its people were traders who claimed to be independent of everyone around them.

Whatever the claim, first Venice, then Hungary, acted as ''protectors'' of the town. They

seemed to let the traders prosper and by the early seventeenth century Ragusa was another word for great wealth among all the seafaring merchants of Europe.

Then came disaster. An earthquake shattered the town and what happened next was similar to what London went through a year or two earlier, in 1665-66. First fire swept through the stricken town. It gutted the cathedral and many of the important buildings. Then came plague, which killed a fifth of the population.

Ragusa could not rebuild with-

out people to help, and so parties of Slavs from the mainland arrived, gradually put the pieces together again, settled down, and called the town by its Slav name of Dubrovnik.

The French arrived in the town in 1806; eight years later it was handed over to the Austria-Hungary Empire. Then came the First World War, in which Austria-Hungary, in its turn, was reduced, and Dubrovnik became part of Yugoslavia.

Its usefulness as a port was recognised by the Italians, who occupied it in 1941, but in 1944 Marshal Tito's forces arrived to liberate the town.

Now the only invaders are tourists who come to spend their fourteen days in a good-natured town whose narrow streets and picture postcard shops make it one of Europe's most pleasant bridges between old and new.

BIRDS IN LEGEND

In many parts of Britain there are folklore tales about what are called "The Seven Whistlers." The "Whistlers" are birds, but the mystical "seven" are not always of the same species in different parts of the country. Sometimes the birds are widgeon (left) which whistle wildly when they fly. Elsewhere the "Seven Whistlers" are said to be curlews, and sometimes they are associated with Brent geese. But whatever or wherever they are, the "Seven Whistlers" are regarded as a sure sign of death. In South Shropshire, the "Whistlers" are six in number, and fly about the world calling for the lost seventh. When this last of the "Whistlers" is found, then, say local folk, the end of the world will come.

All round the coasts of the Old World and among fisherfolk there is the belief that gulls and other sea-going birds are the winged souls of drowned people. In Brittany sea-captains who have treated their crews harshly are believed to change into storm petrels, condemned forever to fly low over the wild seas.

In the story of the Irish Saint Brendan's Voyages told in the Middle Ages, and in many languages, we find a variation of dead people turning into birds. St. Brendan and his companions come upon a strange island on which is a well, and, beside it, a handsome tree filled with numerous and sweet singing white birds. The birds tell St. Brendan that once they were angels and Lucifer was their master. When proud Lucifer fell from Heaven because of his pride, the angels fell, too. But, since their offence was but a small one, Our Lord took pity on them, changed them into birds and set them in the beautiful tree. There they lived without pain, and in eternal joy.

In olden times it was thought that some birds were partly fish, and the barnacle goose (left) was one of those birds believed to have been born from rotting pieces of wood floating in the sea. In 1187 a Welsh historian named Giraldus wrote: "Being at first gummy excrescences from pine-beams floating on the waters, and then enclosed in shells to secure their free growth, they hang by their beaks like seaweed attached to timber. Being in process of time well covered with feathers, they either fall into the water, or take their flight in the free air." The puffin (right) or sea-parrot was also considered to be a "bird-fish", born, like the barnacle geese, from floating wood.

It is the blackbird which is always associated with that well-known Irish man of God, the Blessed St. Kevin. A story goes that during one Lenten season St. Kevin left the company of other men and withdrew to a small and lonely hut. There he contemplated and prayed. During his devotions he had the habit of putting his hands, outstretched, through a small window. One day a blackbird, seeing the hands, proceeded to make a nest in them, and to lay her eggs. St. Kevin, who was always understanding of, and gentle with, all of God's living creations, kept his hands in position until the young birds were hatched and flown.

Saint Werburga of Chester, the daughter of the King of Mercia, took vows as a holy woman. There are many tales of miracles worked by her. In one, the steward of her farm told her that wild geese were eating the standing corn, and nothing would drive them away. "Go and shut them in a house," commanded the saint. The steward, thinking that she was joking, called out to the geese: "The Lady Werburga has ordered you to follow me." The geese bowed their heads and obeyed! He locked them in a barn, all save one which he killed and ate!

Next day at dawn Saint Werburga, after scolding the geese for eating her corn, released them. They circled round and round her feet, complaining. She understood at once what had happened and ordered the steward to bring to her all the bones and feathers of the dead bird. With a healing sign she restored the bird which lived again. The geese thanked Saint Werburga for restoring their companion and took to the air, leaving her corn alone.

THE STRUGGLE

Some while ago, a television company asked for volunteers who would be prepared to live in a remote part of Southern England for one year. The object of the programme was for these men and women to duplicate the conditions under which people of the Iron Age had once existed. The people involved managed to cope well enough with the cold, the mud and the very rough diet that they ate as part of the experiment. But they found themselves all fingers and thumbs when it came to erecting a shelter or building of any sort.

Stone Age man suffered similar problems. He was surrounded on all sides by vast areas of woodlands and forests. However, he did not possess any kind of a tool with a really sharp edge. At first, he chopped doggedly at tree trunks with a large, clumsy, chipped rock but to bring down one large tree might take, perhaps, a month. A new method had to be devised and finally Stone Age man stumbled upon the solution. After much trial and error, he found how to make a tool that would last, instead of splintering in his hands.

As he gazed at his campfire, a small spark stirred in his subconscious. He came to realise that fire, besides consuming, could temper; that is, put a lasting edge on the flint implements he had been using. No longer would he have to scour the limestone cliffs in his neighbourhood for a fresh supply of flints – now he had something that might even outlast his own lifetime. From using his hands, primitive man had begun to use his brain.

But blowing up the fire to make a fierce heat was a tedious business. The Stone Age people came up with a bright idea – artificial lungs; in other words, a pair of bellows that would serve the same purpose. More and more, man was learning how to make inanimate objects work for him. Then he discovered what was to prove just as important as his original discovery – something called a handle.

By tying his precious cutting edge to a length of wood, he could use the tool to greater advantage. Now he found that not only could he cut down trees with greater ease, but that he could make and, what was more, *shape* things to any form he fancied. It was but a short step to the knowledge that

110

The hunters return bringing with them a plentiful supply of meat for the days to come.

Life was hard for Stone Age man. There was the daily problem of finding enough to eat, and the need to find shelter from the elements and wild animals. But gradually man developed the means to help him survive in a hostile world.

FOR SURVIVAL

his cutting edge could be used to hollow out small objects such as bowls and platters to hold food. In his ape-like mind, something began to stir. Wood floated, that he knew, so why should he not make some kind of a craft which he could use to venture upon water?

We can imagine him binding together with vines two or three logs to make the first raft and his first timid attempt to control it. Who knows who began with the first rough adze to hollow out the first boat? Who knows what jeers greeted the Stone Age inventor when he launched it? But it worked and man had added a new dimension to his activities. From watching water animals, such as beavers and otters, he saw that they propelled themselves along with flat-shaped tails and flippers.

Island settlements provided some security from attack.

Slowly, he evolved the idea of paddles which would do the same for him. With the success of his efforts, came growing confidence.

Settling Down

No longer need he cower in caves or huddle about a campfire, afraid to let it grow cold. He set out to make a shelter for himself and his tribe, using the instruments he had devised. With the help of his new-found friend – his trusty axe – he built a crude fence to keep out ferocious animals. Then he decided that the best idea was to build a permanent settlement on an island which would make it harder for enemies – human or otherwise – to reach him. This is just what he did and thousands of years before the Middle Ages and their stone castles, came the moat – a body of water surrounding the main settlement.

Now he had a permanent weapon, a permanent home and a permanent means of transport. In his boat, he could roam the rivers and streams in his immediate neighbourhood. When the supply of food was scarce, he no longer had the spectre of famine staring him in the face. Now he could range further afield and return laden with supplies not just for himself, but for a whole family or community. Man had learned how to live off the land.

His slow-moving but gradually developing process of reasoning led him to another discovery that came with his increasing know-

The first river craft were simply logs which Stone Age man sat astride. Later, when tools were developed, these logs were hollowed out to form a rough form of canoe.

ledge of metals. Two parts of an axe head were cast in moulds and the parts bound together. Then liquid metal was poured in, with a space left for the handle. When the metal had set, the mould was opened and inside was the complete axe-head. Once a handle was fixed, the axe was complete and man had entered . . . the Iron Age.

Stone Age man had learned one basic lesson of life – survival!

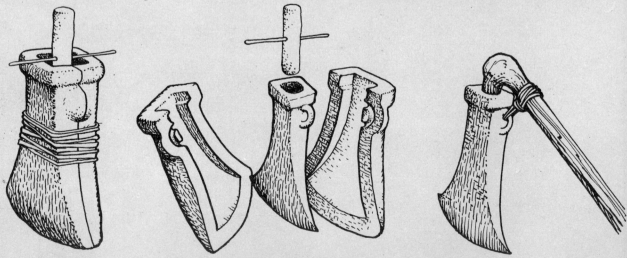

The discovery of metal and its uses meant that man was able to make more sophisticated tools. The method employed in the making of an axe is shown here. First a mould was made in two halves. This was bound together with twine. In order to leave a hole for the handle a clay core was suspended in the centre of the mould. Then hot metal was poured in and left to harden. The two halves of the mould were then separated to reveal the complete axe head. There then remained the task of fixing the handle and the axe was ready for use.

112

TEARS OF THE SUN GOD

Among the many ancient Greek legends about Apollo, son of Zeus and sometimes known as the Sun God, is one which tells of his banishment from Mount Olympus for some misdemeanour, and his sorrow at having to leave his home causing him to weep sun-kissed tears which turned into drops of amber.

The origin of this piece of fiction is unknown, but it may well have been written by an early sculptor or engraver who discovered some pieces of the material now called amber, and found them smooth and pleasant to the touch, and a beautiful soft golden colour, ideal for transforming into works of art.

Over the centuries beautiful works of art have been sculpted or engraved from a variety of substances which are both pleasant to the touch as well as to the eye. Materials such as marble, ivory and jade fall into this category, where pleasure can be obtained from both looking at and feeling the object fashioned by the artist.

Although not particularly valuable, amber is considered by many people to be one of the most unusual and satisfying substances from which to carve small statuettes, make bracelets or necklaces and many other objets d'art. Its origin is certainly unusual.

Countless ages ago vast areas of northern Europe were covered by great forests, and with the passage of time the numerous conifers which predominated over other species of trees, oozed out a pale yellow resin. This sticky material dripped in overlapping rivulets rather like syrup off a spoon, and great heaps of it were gradually covered over by layers of soil.

Over millions of years these buried lumps of resin hardened and changed into what we now know as amber. The result is a brittle yellow-brown translucent substance hard enough to be engraved or cut into beads and other ornaments.

It was highly valued by the ancient Phoenicians, Greeks and Romans who thought it had mysterious healing powers because of its ability to generate static electricity when it is rubbed against a dry cloth. The Greeks called it *elektron*, a word from which our word electricity is derived.

Entomologists – scientists who study insects – are sometimes interested in pieces of amber, because occasionally samples of species long since extinct have been found entombed in them. These insects would have been flying amongst the forest trees millions of years ago, and accidentally become stuck in the oozing resin. Fragments of leaves have also been found embedded in amber.

The type of pine tree which produced amber flourished chiefly in the area now covered by the Baltic Sea and the North Sea, and when violent storms disturb the seabed pieces of amber are often washed ashore. They are usually small in size, but chunks weighing up to 7 kilos have been found.

In ancient times most amber was found in this way, but today supplies are obtained by mining, and about ninety-eight percent comes from the Baltic coastal regions. However, amber is also found in significant quantities in places as far apart as China, Burma, Rumania, Iran and the island of Sicily in the Mediterranean.

Many everyday objects such as umbrella handles, cigarette holders and pipe mouthpieces were once made from amber, but plastics have now largely taken its place for such things, leaving its main use that of providing the material for carved figurines and adornments of various kinds.

Amber will not melt, nor can it be dissolved, but it can be burned when a yellow oil is obtained which gives off a pleasant aroma. Even today this has been used as an inhalant, and there are people who firmly believe that these golden 'Tears of Apollo' can heal sore throats, rheumatism and respiratory conditions such as asthma.

THE TURNING TIDE

Half an hour ago you left the rest of your family to continue their lazy slumbers on the golden stretch of sand alongside the jutting rocks and the cool, silver sea and wander off in search of sea shells and star-fish.

On your return to the beach, you can hardly believe your eyes. They are all still fast asleep, but the radio nearby, and the sun-shade, and the picnic hamper, are in six inches of water! Everyone forgot to take into account the rise and fall of the tides – one of nature's most impressive displays of strength.

Most people who have lived by the sea – or even just paid a short visit whilst on holiday – could hardly fail to have noticed how the waters creep slowly up the beach for about six hours, and then for six hours slip steadily back down again.

The connection of this strange movement with the moon was noted at a relatively early stage in man's development, but until Sir Isaac Newton's discovery of the law of gravity the cause could not be satisfactorily explained. Little wonder that the earliest civilisations paid devout homage to the rise and fall of the tides, thinking they were the work of the gods.

The rise and fall of the tides is now known to be due to the pull of the moon on the earth, sometimes helped and sometimes hindered by the sun, depending on whether these two bodies are in a straight line and pull on the earth together, or pull in different directions. The moon is so much nearer the earth than the sun that, although its mass is not as great, its tide-raising force is more than twice that of the sun.

Whenever the moon rises over the sea, it begins to make its influence felt. The water-mass lying just under it is pulled into a heap by the force of the moon's gravity acting upon it. The centre of this heap of water points directly from the centre of the earth to the centre of the moon. So a great wave is started, travelling across the wide sea, thus making a high tide. Then, by reason of the earth's natural rotation, the peak passes on and the water returns to its own level. This is called the "direct" tide.

There are also the "opposite" tides, which occur at the same time as the direct tides, only on the other side of the earth in a corresponding position. This explains why we have two high tides every 24 hours (or, more exactly, every 24 hours and 49 minutes).

Twice in the course of every month, when the moon is new or full, it comes into line with both the sun and the earth. At these times both the sun and the moon pull together, and the higher tides which result are called "spring" tides – though this description has absolutely no connection with the season of the year. The opposite of this double pulling effect comes near the first and last quarters of the moon's cycle, when the "pulls" of moon and sun are somewhat counterbalanced.

As the sun and the moon pull against each other, with the earth in between, the lifting effect on the world's waters is greatly diminished. The resulting low tides are called "neap" tides – a word which is probably derived from the old English meaning of "nipped".

In the mouths of some rivers, and sometimes in sharply narrowing ocean inlets, the rising of the spring tide occasionally has a curious effect. The tides overcome the current of the

river, and a single high wave, moving onward like a wall of water, rushes with great violence and a roaring noise up the river bed. This sometimes fearsome phenomenon, notable in the rivers Severn and Trent, is called a "bore".

It is not generally known that the rise and fall of the tide varies considerably in different places. In mid-ocean, the difference between high and low water is noticeable only in the vicinity of island shore-lines, where the variation in water levels may only be a couple of metres at most. On the shores of the continents, however, especially in the gradually narrowing bays, the additional depth of water at high tide may be very much larger.

In England, for example, at Newport and Chepstow on the Bristol Channel, the spring tide may rise and fall by as much as twelve metres – no laughing matter to a boat owner who has inadvertantly beached his vessel too low down the sea-shore.

Generally speaking, the tides which occur in lakes and other inland waterways are too small to be noticeable, but it is an interesting fact that the Japanese have developed a scientific device which is so sensitive that it has been able to detect the moon's pull on a cup of tea!

An intimate knowledge of the workings of the tides is of vital importance to the ship's navigator, as a difference of a metre or two in depth may be the deciding factor between staying afloat or running aground on deadly underwater rocks.

It is all a far cry from the family soaking described at the beginning of this story, but the same basic natural principals apply to every aspect of the tale of the tides.

The sea in two vastly different moods. Holiday-makers, above, enjoy the gentle rise and fall of the tide. Below; fierce winds can turn the tide into a fearsome force.

AGE OF INVENTION

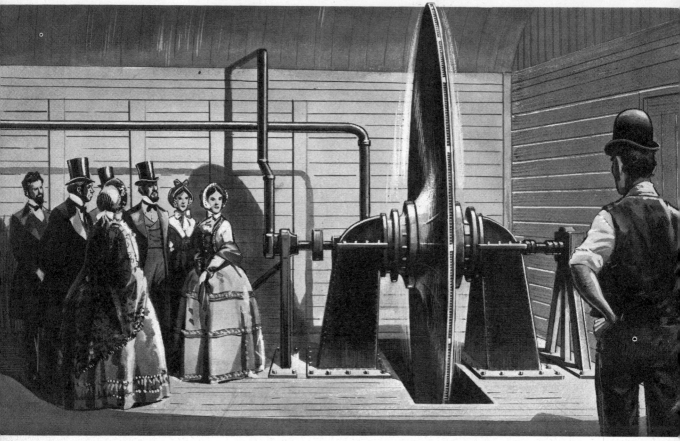

No wonder the Victorian ladies held back in some trepidation when they were taken to see this frightening-looking apparatus. But, they had no need to worry. It was merely a fly-wheel – although a big one – in the engine house of a new plant for keeping the mail flowing.

As it spun to keep an enormous pump operating smoothly, small trains were being sucked through a 762 mm diameter tube running from Euston railway station in London to a sorting office one-third of a mile away.

On its opening day the first mail train reached Euston at 9.45 a.m. Thirty-five mail bags were placed in the tube's long narrow trucks, running on a track, by 9.47 a.m. All of the air in the tube ahead of the trucks was sucked out, making a vacuum. The blast of air behind the trucks, rushing in to fill the vacuum, pushed the train to the sorting office in one minute.

Before they embarked on this project, the Pneumatic Despatch Company, whose brainchild this was, got to work adapting the piston and cylinder principle to locomotion. In this case, the tube becomes the cylinder and the trucks the piston. Tubing was laid down on a spare piece of ground, and curves and gradients were introduced. A speed of about 25 miles an hour was achieved.

Rub, scrub, pound, wring, rinse . . . doing the house-hold laundry was once very hard work. Washing machines have ended all that, thank goodness.

One of the big break-throughs for mechanical washing must have been The Pearson Improved Steam Washing Machine on the right. Even a child could use it, as you can see. When the handle was turned, scoops attached to the drum carried boiling water from the bottom and emptied it on to the clothes. This filled the drum with penetrating steam and forced the dirt out of the clothes.

The Victorians who used this could do a fortnight's washing for a family of eight persons in two hours at a cost of less than 2p for gas and soap.

Behind this machine was the theory that the steam dislodged the dirt and the water carried it away. What a boon it was!

THE COURAGE OF THE CHEVANTE

Somewhere in the jungles of Brazil, said early explorers, white Indians lived in fabulously rich cities. Many men have searched for this lost El Dorado and one of the most famous was Colonel Percy Harrison Fawcett. This six-foot ex-athlete, ex-Artillery officer had an almost mystical love for those Indians untouched by European culture.

In 1925 he set out in search of the survivors of Atlantis, the people of El Dorado. He was convinced that they were the descendants of a mighty but corrupt civilisation that had existed long before the rise of ancient Egypt. He found no white Indians, no fabulous city, just the ferocious Chavante and his own death.

Colonel Fawcett's fabulous Atlantis never existed, but the people of central Brazil still believe that gold and jewels in vast profusion lie somewhere along the Rio das Mortes, the River of Deaths. There certainly was some gold, enough to draw the adventurous or foolhardy

Chavante men are great hunters and often hunt jaguar. These animals are a great menace, particularly at night.

from all over the world, but it was a limited supply. Gangs of desperate miners fought over the spoils. The river, which had first been named the Gentle River by early explorers, earned its new name, the River of Deaths, and through no fault of the Indians.

Nevertheless, the ferocious Chavante tribe did attack miners and certainly tried to stop any settlement or cultivation of their land. Ever since the arrival of the first Portuguese settlers in Brazil, hundreds of years earlier, war with the Indians had dragged on. Two tribes in particular resisted stubbornly and earned themselves a reputation as magnificent jungle warriors. They were the Cherente and the Chavante. They raided Brazilian settlements and in revenge the "sertanejo" or backwoodsmen, mercilessly slaughtered any Indians they caught, men, women and children. Still colonisation progressed and the Indians withdrew westward into the deeper jungles of Amazonia. About the middle of the last century the Cherente tribe found themselves surrounded by white men's villages and had to make peace. But their cousins the Chavante disappeared into the rugged Mato Grosso highlands even farther west. Nothing was heard of them for another fifty years.

People said that they had all died of starvation or been absorbed by other tribes. But they still existed, as Brazilian frontiersmen soon discovered, sixty years ago, when they crossed the raging Araguaia river to be met by a hail of arrows from the jungle ahead.

Even today some of the Chavante refuse to make any contact with the Brazilians. Other Chavante live in an uneasy peace with their settled neighbours. More often than not it is no more than an armed truce. The Indians live in their own way and will permit no interference from the Government. If a settler, gold prospector or Government official tries to bully them, he is likely to end up dead. Even as recently as the mid-1950s a Brazilian Indian Service expedition which set out to study and befriend the Chavante, was wiped out to a man.

All the Chavante, friendly or otherwise, live in villages deep in the Mato Grosso, a sea of grass and stunted trees. Most villages are no more than a circle of domed grass huts. In the middle of the village is an area of beaten earth where the Chavante hold their frequent meetings and dances. The people divide themselves strictly according to age and seniority, each group organising its own complicated ceremonials. The proudest and most magnificent group, or "age set", must be the young warriors. They have gone through their initiation into manhood but are not yet admitted to the tribe's council of elders. Instead they hold their own council in the middle of the village at dusk. Their scarlet war-paint on chest and back, the hawk feathers around their necks and the vicious looking club that each man carries, are enough to scare off most visitors.

To become a man is a tough and lengthy business for a Chavante boy. Those undergoing the initiation have their ears pierced and three-inch wooden cylinders, symbolising manhood, are inserted. For weeks they remain apart from the rest of the village in their own hut. Before dawn and at evening they have to run races, while throughout the day they march in parade around the huts. Almost every night they are again awakened to go singing about the village.

Boys are also taught to hunt, for this is a man's most important task. Chavante hunt tapir and wild pig for food. They also hunt jaguar which are a constant menace, particularly at night. Hunting them is a dangerous business, so before setting out, the men wear specially reddened ear-plugs and perform secret ceremonies to ensure their own safety.

Even those ceremonies before a jaguar hunt seem insignificant compared with a Wai'a. When a Wai'a is held all the women and uninitiated boys are confined to their huts while the men dance and sing in a nearby jungle clearing.

About noon the men march back into the village and once more dance while the women and children cower terrified inside the huts. On the second day of the Wai'a the men return to their forest clearing to

Many attempts have been made to establish friendly relations with the Chavante. But all have ended in failure.

118

All the Chavante live in villages deep in the Mato Grosso, a sea of grass and stunted trees. Most villages are no more than a circle of domed grass huts. Above, women of the Chavante prepare their simple food.

chant a doleful song to the booming of a hollow gourd. The young men who have never before attended a Wai'a are thrust into the middle of the clearing. There they stand motionless, gritting their teeth and staring at the ground while their elders try to scare them or make them move. They dance the terrible death dance, backwards and forwards, so close that they stamp on the young men's feet. This is how the newly initiated prove their manhood, steadfastness and nerve. This is the courage that still enables the Chavante to hold their own in a cold, wet and rugged landscape and against the ever-encroaching Brazilian settlers.

As they reached the river, the men were greeted by a hail of arrows.

TO GET TO THE OTHER SIDE...

The 15th century bridge at Bidford-on-Avon.

Have you ever thought how often you cross over, walk under or walk near a bridge, and usually just take it as a matter of course, feeling it has been put there for your convenience to ride or walk over?

Yet many bridges have little known and unusual features in their make-up which are well worth looking at when it is possible to stop and examine them properly.

The bridge over the River Tweed at Kelso, in Scotland, was built by the famous engineer John Rennie in 1803, and was used as a prototype for his bridge over the Thames at Waterloo which he commenced to build in 1811.

When this Waterloo Bridge was demolished during the 1930s and 1940s, two of its lamps were removed and you can now see these old relics of London fixed to the bridge at Kelso.

Not so far. away to the east, between Norham and Berwick-on-Tweed, in Northumberland, the Union Bridge crossing the River Tweed can be found. It was constructed by Sir Samuel Brown in 1826, and was the earliest large suspension bridge in England.

Further south, at Alnwick, Northumberland, is the Lion Bridge (dated 1773), which previously had a unicorn on one side, and a lion (which still remains) on the other; but the unicorn had to be removed because, it is said, it frightened too many horses which were ridden or driven over the bridge.

Near to the place where the unicorn used to be, "Fox's Leap" is carved, which marks the spot where Fox, a militia deserter under escort, leapt over the parapet and escaped.

There will not be enough space to mention many of the fine packhorse bridges which can still be seen in a number of places, but it is worth going a long way to see the fine double-arched example at Wycollar in Lancashire, and for extra interest there is nearby Wycollar Hall which is thought to be the setting for 'Ferndean' in Charlotte Brontës *Jane Eyre*.

An interesting bit of an old bridge at South Kilvington, North Yorkshire, which was demolished for road widening is visible on the new bridge. It is known as the "Fiddle Stone" because it is shaped like a violin, and it was probably carved by a wandering musician during the 19th century.

At Congleton, Cheshire, you can see something really unique in bridge construction. The remarkable "Snake" bridge over the canal has been designed so that the towpath is taken both over and under it, which makes the detaching of towlines unnecessary.

Moving across to Lincolnshire, the famous 13th century triangular bridge at Crowland was once described as "the greatest curiosity in Britain if not in Europe".

It is in the centre of the town, and when you stand on it you might well

One of the many bridges spanning the River Thames can be seen at Kingston-Upon-Thames.

say "Where is the water?", but once the streets were waterways which have since receded a considerable distance. In fact, it is known that both Henry VI and Edward IV (on his way to Fotheringhay Castle) landed at the bridge.

The Old Bridge at Llanrwst, Gwynedd, was built by Inigo Jones in 1636, and although it looks rather massive a story has long been in existence that if it is bumped in a certain way it will vibrate.

A guide book of 1868 tells us that a man was specially employed to ask visitors if they wished to "have a shake".

Do not pass over the unusual 15th century bridge at Bidford-on-Avon, Warwickshire, without first having a look at its eight arches, and you will see that each one is of different shape, height and span from the others.

You are almost bound to visit Cambridge at some time or other, and whilst you are there remember to look for the wooden bridge which spans the River Cam at Queen's College.

The first bridge was constructed in 1749 on mathematical principles which meant that not one nail was needed in its make-up, and the present bridge was built at the beginning of this century on similar lines. See if you can spot a nail in it!!

The railway bridge over the River Thames at Maidenhead, Berkshire, was built by Brunel, and it is thought to have the largest and flattest arches ever constructed in brick.

If you stand under it on the Buckinghamshire side of the river and make a noise you may be able to hear a nine times repeated echo.

There is an interesting, small, late 12th century three arched

bridge to be seen at Kingston-Upon-Thames, Surrey. Known as the Clattern Bridge, it spans the little Hogsmill River, and from it nagging wives used to be thrown into the water.

Should you visit London's Zoo remember to look out for the site of "Blow-up" Bridge which can be found near the Macclesfield Gate of Regent's Park.

One day in 1874 gunpowder loaded on a passing barge exploded and practically demolished Macclesfield Bridge as it was then called, but it was re-erected, and if you look closely at the supporting pillars you can see the groove marks made by the ropes which were attached to the barges.

To conclude, here is rather an improbable tale about a bridge which can be seen spanning a tributary of the River Brede at Brede in East Sussex. It is known locally as the "Groaning Bridge".

It seems that Sir Goddard Oxenbridge (whose stone figure can be seen in the church) was an ogre who killed and ate small children.

Apparently, he could only be killed by being sawn in half with a wooden saw, and one day the children of the neighbourhood managed to drug him and cut him in two with a huge wooden saw with the young people of West Sussex at one end, and those of East Sussex at the other.

This all happened at the "Groaning Bridge", and it is said that Sir Goddard's groans can occasionally be heard there at midnight.

There are many more bridges of various types to be found up and down Great Britain so search them out with the aid of local guide books, or reference librarians and you will build up a collection of fascinating little tales which will make your future outings and holidays much more interesting.

BOXING CLEVER

by Andy Davies

When assembling the nestbox panel pins can be used to hold the pieces in position until they can be secured with screws.

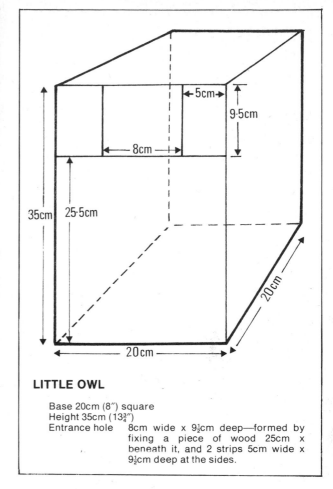

LITTLE OWL

Base 20cm (8″) square
Height 35cm (13¾″)
Entrance hole   8cm wide x 9½cm deep—formed by fixing a piece of wood 25cm x beneath it, and 2 strips 5cm wide x 9½cm deep at the sides.

Inspired by nestbox success with blue tits and other small birds, some friends and I thought we would try our hand at making nestboxes for larger birds—the birds of prey—but we found it was not so easy. For one thing, we found that while nestboxes for the small passerines could be put up in a fairly haphazard manner and still be used, it was clear that the birds of prey were not the slightest bit interested in a badly-positioned nestbox. This meant observation, study and research. The other stumbling block was that we could not find any published information about the measurements and materials required for these larger boxes, and this meant finding out by trial and error.

At first, our new venture failed miserably, which disappointed us after the earlier successes; but it also made us all the more determined to succeed, especially as many of the old elm trees were being cut down in the interests of public safety, taking many natural nesting-holes with them.

We worked on the project for several years, achieving first one success, then another, and then another, until finally we decided that we must have discovered most of the important factors governing their size and siting. The purpose of this article is to offer readers what we were denied—background information, measurements and tips from someone with experience in the same field.

We believe that the key to the whole business is to discover the birds' favourite trees, and during the autumn or winter months climb up and place nestboxes in them, taking care to position nestboxes appropriate to the size of the bird in question.

Site-hunting can take place for owls during the same months as positioning the boxes (between September and February) although kestrels must be researched in the spring. The reason for this can best be illustrated by

describing some of my own observations and conclusions from earlier this year.

Kestrels like to sit fairly high up in an old or dead tree to survey the land around them for signs of movement. Numerous times during spring I saw a male kestrel in the same oak tree, which although not dead had some dead branches right at the top. Droppings subsequently confirmed that the bird always used the same branch. During the autumn, however, the kestrel was never seen in this tree because the leaves and acorns were very thick, despite the dead branches, and he had found another tree without leaves, from which he could survey his domain unhindered.

The tree I chose for the nestbox was the oak, because at the crucial stage when the young hatch next year, the leaves will once again be coming out and will afford welcome cover to the kestrels. This particular tree should also be safe from human interference because of its height, the difficulty of climbing it in the early stages, and the fact that dead branches tend to put people off even though in this case they are as strong as the living branches. Squirrels, too, should be deterred from this oak because of the absence of nearby trees whose branches they could use as a means of escape, if disturbed.

Obviously many considerations such as the birds' safety have to be thought about before a nestbox of any sort should be erected, but this is especially so with the birds of prey. If, for instance, you are placing a nestbox on farmland (with the owner's consent of course) it is worth bearing in mind that whilst the majority of today's farmers have the right attitude to birds of prey, they may not be the only interested parties. Quite a large number have gamekeepers, or fee-paying shooting syndicates, who may still harbour the old misguided grudges against any bird with a hooked beak.

It may therefore pay, before positioning a nestbox, to do a little discreet research into these attitudes. Although protected by the law, it can still be very difficult to prove that these birds have suffered at the hands of man, and it is safer to prevent any such event rather than cause it.

The owls are perhaps a little easier to locate than the kestrel, although it is sometimes difficult to decide on the exact tree straight away. The two major problems are that you are working in the dark, and the owls' calls have an unusual quality about them which, if heard from close to, could be coming from anywhere.

Tawny owls, being birds that prefer woods, are the more difficult in this respect than little owls, who normally do not have the same choice of cover. The technique with the latter is to observe the inhabited copse over a period of several evenings from a good distance. This clarifies the observer's idea of the exact source of the calls, especially when backed up by using different observation-points on successive nights.

The nature of the terrain will probably call for some variation of this technique when applied to tawny owls, which could only be decided upon by the features of the landscape in question.

Building the nestboxes is the next move, and we generally use strong plywood (Marine plywood is ideal) which surrounds a framework of wooden offcuts, preferably square (2cm or thereabouts). The boxes last longer if coated with preservative and then a coat of green paint. Not that the colour will make any difference to the birds—this is once again to camouflage the nestbox from human interest. If time or materials are not available we put the boxes up as they are. A layer of roofing felt, if access to this is possible, has also helped prolong our nestboxes in the past. Panel pins are initially used, to hold the various pieces in position, which are then secured with screws. I have given on these pages the exact dimensions of our successful kestrel and little owl nestboxes, but have not given details for tawny owls because these seem to use almost any size and shape so long as it is large enough.

One of our most successful tawny owl boxes is an old, wooden, 9-gallon beer barrel, with half of one end knocked out. Not the half with the bung hole in it, because this provided a good place to insert a branch for the bird to perch on just below the hole.

Hauling the nestboxes up trees can be difficult—even dangerous—but by wedging a stick in the nestbox as shown in the picture, the method will be simple and safe. Finally, we spread a thin layer of the litter found below the tree over the bottom of the inside of the nestbox, as we find the birds of prey are more likely to be tempted to use the box than if it were left bare. Leaves should be avoided, as these will tempt squirrels.

After a nestbox has been occupied, the soiled litter should be removed and replaced with a clean layer. Do this sufficiently long before the next breeding season to allow for the same amount of weathering and seasoning to take place as you would with a new nestbox.

It is a thrilling experience to make and successfully postiton one of these larger nestboxes, although instant success should not be anticipated. The important thing is not to be discouraged if things do not immediately go well. Most nestbox-rejections are due to some small siting fault, which can usually be discovered by comparing it to a natural hole which has proved more enticing to the birds.

But it should be borne in mind that natural holes, too, may be ignored for several years before use, and even after use are often interchanged with other holes. You may find your nestbox being occupied by a bird for which it was not intended, in which case you will be in good company.

The Michigan Audobon Society apparently erected platforms on pylons for Ospreys—and had them used by Bald Eagles, which just proves how unpredictable—and therefore exciting—this can be. We wish you luck with your nestboxes, and hope you find their occupants as fascinating as we have done.

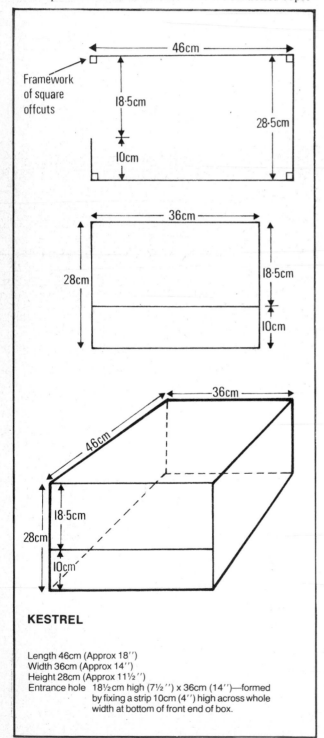

KESTREL

Length 46cm (Approx 18'')
Width 36cm (Approx 14'')
Height 28cm (Approx 11½'')
Entrance hole   18½cm high (7½'') x 36cm (14'')—formed
by fixing a strip 10cm (4'') high across whole
width at bottom of front end of box.

TAWNY OWL

Almost any size and shape, as long as box big enough. Dimensions must be at least those for the kestrel nestbox, and double this size is not too large. The hole can be any shape (square, rectangular, semi-circular, to mention but a few of the successful ones I know about) and can be positioned at the top, at the edge, or in the middle. Ideal nestbox is a wooden, 9-gallon beer barrel laid on its side, and half of one end knocked out.

DEATH OF A GERMAN GIANT

I**T was a warm evening in a South American port, with crowds lining the quay watching a ship preparing to leave. A scene that is repeated thousands of times every year in harbours all over the world. But this time it was different. The ship that was about to leave was the pride of Adolf Hitler's reconstituted German Navy, the pocket battleship called the *Admiral Graf Spee*.

For the beginning of this momentous story we have to go back four months from the day of the incident – back to August 21st, 1939. The port of Wilhelmshaven saw the departure of the most lethal weapon in the German naval arsenal. The *Graf Spee* was a unique class of warship. With her 11-inch guns and heavy armour, she could out-range and out-gun any English vessel able to match her speed of nearly 30 knots. And, with that sort of speed, she could out-run any of the English battleships that might threaten her and try to engage her in battle.

Lone Wolf

The mission of the *Graf Spee*, and her Captain, Hans Langsdorff, was to harry and destroy Allied shipping, wherever in the world they might be encountered. With her own free-ranging support vessel – the *Altmark* – to keep her armed and provisioned, and to look after her prisoners, the *Graf Spee* was an immensely dangerous lone wolf of the seas.

Between the 12th September, when she first entered the shipping lanes of the South Atlantic, and the 13th December, she captured and sank nine merchant vessels. During these operations not one Allied seaman lost his life – a remarkable humanitarian achievement by Captain Langsdorff.

It was on 13th December, off the coast of Uruguay, that destiny caught up with the lean grey shape of the *Graf Spee*. The Admiralty had known for weeks that at least one, and possibly two, German surface raiders were loose. A light cruiser squadron, under the command of the brilliant strategist Commodore

The whole world waited with baited breath for news of the fate of the *Graf Spee* and her crew. For Captain Langsdorff the loss of his ship proved too much . . .

Harwood, was off the South American coast, attempting a difficult intercept operation. Harwood had guessed that the captain of the German ship would try one last attack in that area. It was that stroke of genius that was to doom the *Graf Spee*.

The British squadron consisted of the cruisers *Ajax*, which flew Harwood's broad commodore's pennant, *Exeter* and the New Zealand vessel – H.M.N.Z.S. *Achilles*. Just after five o'clock in the morning of the 13th, the squadron encountered the pocket battleship. The Battle of the River Plate lasted nearly two and a half hours and ended in a clear victory for the Allied cause. Although the *Exeter* had been badly damaged and had broken off the action in a

desperate bid to reach the safety of the Falkland Islands base (she made it successfully), both *Ajax* and *Achilles* were relatively undamaged. The *Graf Spee*, with 65 hits on the superstructure alone, and with dead and dying below decks, had broken off the action and slunk for the neutral port of Montevideo, where she arrived, showing no lights, later that night.

The next two days were a furious round of diplomatic action. Under International Law, neutral nations were required to render assistance to damaged warships putting into their ports. But, and here was the nub of the problem, there was a rigid time-limit. Despite all Langsdorff's pleas, the Uruguayan government laid down that the *Graf Spee* should leave by eight o'clock

on the evening of Sunday, 17th December.

Time passed all too quickly. The English cruisers, joined now by the old *Cumberland* patrolled outside the harbour. By a magnificent counter-espionage ruse, the Germans were tricked into thinking that the British ships in the estuary of the River Plate included the capital vessels the *Ark Royal* and the *Renown*.

Neat Move

Essential repairs were carried out and the world waited with bated breath to see what the Germans would do. Surely they wouldn't just submit tamely till the deadline had passed and their prize ship was interned for the duration of the war.